ADVANTAGE WHITE AND MALE, DISADVANTAGE BLACK AND FEMALE

ADVANTAGE WHITE AND MALE, DISADVANTAGE BLACK AND FEMALE

Income Inequality, Economic Well-Being, and Economic Mobility Among Families in a Youth Cohort, 1979-1993

Richard K. Caputo, Ph.D.

Rutledge Books, Inc. Danbury, CT

Rutledge Books, Inc.
107 Mill Plain Road, Danbury, CT 06811
1-800-278-8533
www.rutledgebooks.com

Manufactured in the United States of America

Cataloging-in-Publication Data
Caputo, Richard K.
Advantage white and male, disadvantage black and female: income inequality, economic well-being, and economic mobility among families in a youth cohort, 1979-1993

ISBN: 1-58244-030-1

1. Households -- United States. 2. Cost and standard of living -- United States. 3. Sex discrimination in employment -- United States.

304.6 99-64941

◆ To My Parents ◆

CONTENTS

TABLES

FIGURES

ACKNOWLEDGMENTS

I wish to thank Mary Cianni, Elane Nuehring, and Sharron Singleton-Bowie for their helpful comments on earlier versions of this manuscript. I also thank the anonymous reviewers and panel discussants and participants who critiqued preliminary portions of the manuscript presented at national conferences, as well as those who encouraged expansion of earlier related work. Invariably, I incorporated some suggestions and rejected others, so I accept full responsibility for all shortcomings in the present manuscript.

PREFACE

In this monograph I report a study that examined income inequality, economic well-being, and economic mobility among families of a youth cohort. I wanted to find out how well a cohort of youth fared as they were entering the labor market and forming their own families during the Reagan and Bush presidential administrations and at the beginning of the Clinton administration. Throughout the 1980s and early 1990s, a consensus emerged about the increased importance attributed to the role of personal responsibility about work, its rewards, and family life. In addition, although there was much talk about government's role in the economy and society, increased reliance on market incentives to expand the economy and to encourage greater work effort among all able-bodied adults became operative norms in many social policy debates.

This study spanned a 15-year period during which the political economy of the New Deal welfare state came under attack on ideological and programmatic grounds. Essentially, the public was admonished to expect less from government and rely more on ourselves and on the private sector in matters of economic well-being. The message regarding government was basically negative, a steady drumbeat of claims that the New Deal and Great Society initiatives had gone awry. The message regarding personal responsibility and work effort, however, was optimistic, a cacophonous chorus of market strategies to reward work effort and to expand the economy.

As I read and heard so much about the rich getting richer and the poor getting poorer during the 1980s and 1990s, I wondered to what extent this was the case for those who were entering the work force and forming their own families during this period. I had particular concerns about poor families, about how they fared in an expanding economy in both absolute and relative terms. To what extent did their level of economic well-being mirror the economy? Did their quality of life increase as the economy expanded? Did greater or lesser numbers of families experience poverty, at what magnitude, and for what duration?

I also had an interest in learning about how the economic well-being of these young families varied by sex and ethnicity/race throughout the period. Despite strides in work opportunities and pay equity across sex and ethnicity/race lines since the mid-1960s, there has been much recent debate about whether we have come far enough along to diminish, if not end, the role of affirmative action programs. Is there sufficient evidence to support justifications for complete reliance on market mechanisms to bridge whatever gaps remain? To what extent do whites in general and white men in particular retain privileged positions economically? That is, are they better able to take advantage of shifts in the political economy toward greater reliance on market-based mechanisms and the loosening of government interventions?

It was my hope that examining a youth cohort maturing during the 1980s and early 1990s would provide insight into what other youth cohorts, as well as this one, might expect in an economy increasingly dominated by market principles. To the extent that maturing youth in an expanding economy face greater income disparity, diminished economic well-being, or lack of mobility, in varying degrees by sex and ethnicity/race, justification can be found for redistributive and affirmative action principles associated with the welfare state as we have come to know it since the New Deal of the 1930s.

As the title of this volume suggests, economic privilege still prevails. Although the Reagan promise of improved economic well-being was fulfilled by all sex and ethnicity/race groups in the cohort, including black women and black men, whites in general and white men in particular started out advantaged, did better over time, and were more likely to lock themselves into higher levels of economic well-being. Consistent with Reagan-like claims about causes of economic well-being, strong beliefs in self-determination and individual initiative paid off; not, however, among those economically better off, but among the most economically disadvantaged group in the study, namely black women. In addition, contrary to much popular and political rhetoric about how the Aid to Families with Dependent Children program encouraged and prolonged poverty, receipt of welfare benefits had no effect beyond that of other factors on the economic mobility of black women. However, participation in the much less controversial Food Stamps program did. Education and work effort, particularly full-time employment, contributed the most to economic well-being and economic mobility among black women. In light of these and other findings, I argue for affirmative action work-related strategies aimed at maturing black women whom, of all sex and ethnicity/race groups in the study, the expanding economy of the 1980s and 1990s virtually ignored.

Chapter 1
INCOME INEQUALITY

Introduction

This study focuses on a national sample of American youth aged 14 to 22 in 1979. It seeks to ascertain who among these youth were more or less likely to get ahead and gain some measure of success through actions and means under their own control-in short, to partake of the American Dream-throughout the 1980s and early 1990s (Schwarz, 1997). In doing so, the study examines how social, psychological, demographic, and economic variables influenced the economic well-being of the youth in the cohort. Three empirically-based chapters address income inequality between the most affluent and poorest families, economic well-being among all families, and economic mobility, also among all families, but with particular attention to those families entering and escaping poverty annually between 1979 and 1993. Income inequality and economic well-being have received much attention in the literature, while economic mobility has yet to receive extensive treatment. This study is intended in part to fill this gap. It initially treats income inequality, economic well-being, and economic mobility separately. However, the logic behind the analyses in this chapter and the next form the basis of the third chapter dealing with economic mobility. The final chapter discusses labor- and welfare-reform policies in light of study findings. At issue, given the current climate of opinion about self-sufficiency, the role of government, and affirmative action programs, is whether living in white families, particularly for males, still has its privileges and, to the extent it does, what might be done about it.

Throughout the 1990s, scholars and public officials have focused on stagnant median wages and income inequality as main factors contributing to a diminished American Dream and fueling the public's anxieties about their ability to improve their standard of living in a changing economy (e.g., Bok, 1994; Caputo, 1995a and b; Carnoy, 1994; Krugman, 1992; Levy and Michel, 1991; Levy, 1995; Madrick, 1995; Newman, 1988 and 1993; Phillips, 1993; Reich, 1997). Relying primarily on U.S. Bureau of the Census reports, Zill and Nord (1994), for example, noted little change in the overall growth in real earnings between 1983 and 1992, despite an increase in the ratio of full-time female to male median weekly earnings from 67% to 75%. They attributed women's relative gains in earnings to more years of schooling and work experience than in years past. Also relying on census data, McLanahan and Casper (1995) found that increases in women's earning power accounted for 70% of the decline of marriage among whites aged 25 to 29 between 1970 and 1990, while decreases in men's earning power accounted for only 8% of the decline. Among blacks, neither changes in women's nor men's earning power accounted for the substantial drop in marriage rates during the 1980s or 1990s. McLanahan and Casper noted that the census data failed to say whether changes in attitudes and values were related to marriage rates. They nonetheless speculated that to the extent such changes were important, they were likely to be more important among blacks than among whites.

Karoly (1993) has summarized the major controversies surrounding the increase of income inequality and economic well-being throughout the 1980s in both the popular press and academic literature. In a comprehensive study using annual data on earnings and family income from the March 1964 through March 1990 Current Population Survey (CPS) computer tapes, Karoly concluded that inequality has been increasing on all measures and that the relative economic status of families in the bottom of the income distribution has been falling for almost two decades. The 1980s were unique in the sense of relative gains of the rich, a theme popularized by Phillips (1990). More recently, Danziger and Gottschalk (1995) corroborated Karoly's findings. They showed that in 1969 the poorest 10% of individuals lived in families where the ratio of family income to the poverty line was .39; for the richest 10%, the ratio of family income to the poverty line was 8.39 times the poverty line. In 1991 the poorest 10% of individuals lived in families where the income-to-poverty ratio was .47; for the richest 10%, the ratio of family income to the poverty line was 10.47 times the poverty line.

In a related study accounting for changes in the economic well-being of children between 1968 and 1986, Danziger and Gottschalk (1993) also used CPS data. They limited their samples to women under the age of 55 who were the head of a household or the spouse of a household head. Danziger and Gottschalk focused on the influence of economic and demographic factors on summary measures of resources available to families with children, such as mean total family income and the child poverty rate. They found that increased poverty among children, resulting from increases in female-headed households and income inequality, was offset by declines in family size and increased educational attainment of women.

Findings from research that relied on Panel Study of Income Dynamics (PSID) data (Coe, 1981; Duncan, 1984; Duncan, et al., 1995; Gottschalk, McLanahan, and Sandefur, 1994) also have a bearing on the present study. First, there was no evidence that initial attitudes regarding achievement motivation, sense of personal efficacy, or orientation toward the future affected subsequent economic success. Second, changes in family composition accounted the most for variations in family income. For women this meant that separation and/or divorce drove women into poverty, whereas marriage enabled them to escape. Neither marriage nor divorce had much effect on the incomes of male-headed households, but the birth of a child did. Births reduced the work hours of wives and increased family needs.

Relying on data from a variety of sources, such as the CPS and PSID, and synthesizing decades of academic research, including her own, Blank (1997) documented the difficulty of many American workers to earn wages and benefits adequate to sustain a family. She cited two main reasons why people become poor: Either their families change composition in ways that threaten their economic security, or there is a major economic loss, usually in earnings. Of the two reasons, changes in economics created more poverty than changes in family composition. Likewise, most people escaped poverty when a change occurred in their family's economic resources. In most cases, poverty ended because either the earnings of the head or the spouse increased enough. Increases in government assistance ended 16% of poverty spells. About 13% of poverty spells ended with major changes in who heads the family-either a couple got married, or a child in a poor family left and established an autonomous family. In part reflecting her concern for a variety of "reform" measures that eventually made their way into what became the Personal Responsibility and Work Opportunity Reconciliation Act of 1996, Blank stressed the importance of economic opportunities and the ability of poor adults to find and hold jobs. She noted that contrary to popular belief and, by extension, to findings from some scholarly studies (e.g., Wilson, 1996), there was little evidence that fewer jobs were available for less-skilled workers now compared to twenty years ago. In short, workers with lower levels of education, particularly those from minority racial or ethnic backgrounds, have always faced unemployment rates of 10% or higher. Although this indicates ongoing problems for these workers locating jobs, such problems seem about the same as they were fifteen years ago. Hence, job availability for low-skilled workers remains problematic, for the most part reflecting business cycles, but no more or less so over the long haul.

While Blank (1997 and 1995) highlighted the comparable availability of jobs for low-skilled workers, Burtless (1995) documented the diminished prospects of economic well-being associated with low-wage jobs. In a study using data from the National Longitudinal Survey of Youth (NLSY), which is also the basis of the present study, Burtless showed that unskilled and semi-skilled women's wages had fallen sharply in real terms since 1979. Young female high school dropouts earned nearly 20% less in 1989 than their counterparts in 1979. The prospects of these young women did not improve as they matured: wages increased by only 1.2% a year between the ages of 21 and 29. To the extent that economic well-being was tied to wages, Burtless's findings suggest that the growing economy of the 1980s largely bypassed low-skilled women workers despite the availability of jobs.

Several contemporary studies, though less directly related to the present study because they focused more on self-sufficiency per se, highlighted the influence of attitudes on poverty, use of public assistance, and work effort. In a study of New York and Chicago, Goodwin (1983), for example, sought to determine why some people continually relied on public assistance, whether as participants in the Work Incentive Program (WIN) or as beneficiaries of Unemployment Insurance (UI), while others became independent. Essentially,

Goodwin found that as persons fail to achieve economic independence through work, their expectations of achieving such independence are lowered, in turn lessening their pursuit of employed work. The observed apathy among poor men and the larger number of welfare households headed only by mothers emerged from the inability of these persons to locate jobs. Dolinsky, Caputo, and O'Kane (1989) examined the relative influence of culture and situation on welfare receipt among a nationally representative sample of matched mother-daughter pairs. They found that both culture and situation influenced inter-generation welfare receipt, but that education and work experience were about three times as important as attitudes in explaining the variance in the number of years welfare was received. Cultural and attitudinal factors included measures of orientation to family life, locus of control, and views toward women working outside the home (also, see Joe, 1971).

Focusing on inner-city poverty, three recent projects, the Chicago Urban Poverty and Family Life Study (UPFLS), the Oakland and Woodland Neighborhood Study, and the Effects of Neighborhoods on Adolescent Social Outcomes, conducted at the Center for the Study of Urban Inequality at the University of Chicago, also highlighted the inter-relatedness of social psychological attributes, as well as socio-demographic factors, on joblessness and family formation (Wilson, 1996). UPFLS findings showed that individuals residing in poor neighborhoods in Chicago adhered to many work-related values consistent with the dominant American belief system concerning poverty and individual initiative. Although the UPFLS was not a longitudinal study, it collected retrospective (or life history) marriage and employment data that allowed the estimation of trends. Findings revealed that marriage rates dropped more markedly among jobless black fathers than among employed black fathers. This drop, however, applied only to the younger cohorts. Employment increased the likelihood of marriage by eight times for UPFLS single fathers ages 18 to 31, while having no significant effect on the likelihood that UPFLS single fathers ages 32 to 44 would eventually marry. Wilson concluded that joblessness multiplied the effects of poverty on family formation and structure, i.e., as inner-city employment prospects receded, the foundation for stable relationships became weaker over time beyond the effects attributable to poverty alone.

In some of my earlier work, I too examined the relationship between psychological and attitudinal attributes and poverty dynamics and economic well-being. Like the present study, my earlier ones relied on the National Longitudinal Survey of Youth (NLSY), a nationally representative sample of noninstitutionalized youth in the U.S. aged 14 to 22 in 1979. In the study most directly related to the present one (Caputo, 1998), I examined socio-demographic and psychological correlates of economic well-being for two subsets of the youth cohort, namely those 22 years of age and older in 1979 and in 1987. Results indicated that education, hours worked, and marital status were the most consistent predictors of economic well-being depending on the sex and ethnicity/race of respondents in study years 1985 and 1992, while self-esteem was also a consistent predictor among Hispanic men and white women in 1992, the most recent year of data available at the time of that study. Nonetheless, the influence of education on economic well-being declined between 1985 and 1992 for all groups except white women, while the influence of hours worked declined for all groups except Hispanic women and black men.

The study noted above (Caputo, 1998) also examined income inequality within the cohort in 1980, compared it to 1992, and found that the percentage of respondents who lived in poor families declined, but at different rates when accounting for sex and ethnicity/race.

Poverty rates declined most for males in general and for white males in particular, although Hispanic females fared somewhat better than their male counterparts. In addition, the percentage of respondents who lived in rich families increased for all groups except black and Hispanic women, while the increase for white women was below that of men regardless of ethnicity/race. These findings suggested that, although the percentages of respondents who lived in poor families shrunk while those who lived in rich families proportionately increased, young men fared better than young women as they matured over the study period. Finally, in regard to changes in economic well-being between 1980 and 1992 by sex and ethnicity/race, the study found that each group improved. However, when accounting for all respondents in the aggregate, women fared better, depending on ethnicity/race, than when considering only those who lived in poor or rich families. Among all groups, white men again fared best, having the highest level of economic well-being, as well as maintaining their relative position, between 1980 and 1992, but white women also did as well as black and Hispanic males. Black women fared the worst. Their level of economic well-being was lowest and remained that way throughout the study period.

Two other of my earlier studies using the NLSY data focused on poverty dynamics, namely escaping poverty and achieving self-sufficiency (Caputo, 1997) and becoming poor and using public assistance programs (Caputo, 1999). In both works, I assessed the influence of psychological and attitudinal attributes beyond that of socio-demographic factors on dynamics at the lower end of the income scale between 1991 and 1992. As was the case in many of the studies cited previously, socio-demographic factors were far more influential in affecting poverty dynamics than were psychological and attitudinal attributes. Due to the longitudinal nature of the NLSY, however, I incorporated several cumulative variables, such as the number of years in poverty, and change variables, such as change in the number of hours worked between 1991 and 1992. The cumulative variables proved highly predictive of poverty dynamics, eclipsing even human capital variables such as educational level. The first of these two studies found that the number of years respondents lived in poverty was the best predictor of escaping poverty, while the number of years respondents made use of public assistance programs was the best predictor of becoming self-sufficient. In addition, marital status and change in the number of hours worked between 1991 and 1992 influenced the prospect for escaping poverty, though not becoming self-sufficient. Likewise, the second study found that the number of years respondents lived in poverty was the best predictor of moving from above poverty in one year to below poverty the following year, while the number of years respondents lived in families that received public assistance was the best predictor of moving from self-support to entering into a public assistance program from one year to the next.

Previous research has presented a mixed picture regarding income inequality, poverty dynamics, and economic well-being. As noted, both Blank (1997) and Karoly (1993) described and summarized much of the earlier related scholarship, highlighting variations in purpose, data sources, samples, measures, and designs across studies. On the whole, researchers have demonstrated that, in addition to the state of the economy, demographic characteristics such as educational attainment, family structure and, to a lesser extent ethnicity/race, affect income inequality and economic well-being and that social psychological and personality-related attributes have little if any effect. Duncan (1984) found little evidence for the influence of attitudes. Dolinsky, et al. (1989) found that both culture and situation contributed to poverty, with human capital and socio-demographic factors outweighing attitudinal factors in regard to time spent on welfare. Wilson (1996) found that the likelihood of finding work shaped attitudes about prospects for self-sufficiency, like Goodwin (1983), and also that for younger, poor, urban males joblessness affected their likelihood of marriage. Blank (1997) and Burtless (1995) stressed the importance of labor market conditions and, as did Duncan, et al. (1995), Danziger and Gottschalk (1993), Gottschalk, McLanahan, and Sandefur (1994), and Levy and Michel (1991), family composition and human capital variables on economic well-being and poverty dynamics.

My previous studies focusing on the youth cohort used for present purposes also found that socio-demographic factors were better predictors than psychological attributes of poverty dynamics and economic well-being, although self-esteem was found for some subgroups. The number of years living in poor families was also found to be the best predictor of poverty dynamics. For the most part, economic well-being improved for the cohort as it matured throughout the 1980s. It should be noted, however, that time-related studies vary in part by the nature of samples used and comparisons made: (1) Studies comparing results of samples of individuals drawn from a population at a specified point in time T (for example, T = 1979) and with certain characteristics of interest (for example, age groups 41-50, 51-60) are cross-sectional; (2) Trend studies report results of comparisons between samples of individuals having specified characteristics (for example, age 41-50) drawn from populations at different times (for example, T1 = 1979 and T2 = 1989); (3) Cohort studies compare a sample of individuals having specified characteristics (for example, at age 41-50) drawn from a population at one point in time (say, T1 = 1979) with those of another sample (for example, at age 51-60) drawn at a second point in time (say, T2 = 1989); and (4) Panel studies resemble cohort studies with the significant difference being that the same individuals are followed and reported on at T1 (say, at age 41-50 in 1979) and T2 (say at age 51-60 in 1989). CPS studies were primarily cross-sectional or trend in nature, while users of PSID data had aspects of both trend and panel studies.

In my youth cohort study of income inequality and economic well-being (Caputo, 1998), the reported trends between 1980 and 1992 and between 1985 and 1992 respectively had the characteristics of a panel study. The present study in part extends much of the extant time-related literature by taking advantage of the longitudinal, annually collected nature of the NLSY panel data file. There are a sufficient number of annual snapshots or data points (15) to make use of time series analysis feasible to determine trends in income inequality, poverty dynamics, and economic well-being of the youth cohort. In addition, the retention rate of 89.2% (n = 8,891) in 1994, the last survey year of released data at the time of this study, was considered well within acceptable limits. For the most part, only respondents in the 1994 sample for whom requisite annual information was available since 1979 were included in this study, yielding a usable sample of 2,745 respondents. To minimize loss of cases, mean values were substituted for missing annual family income stratified by sex and ethnicity/race.

As with my previous studies, however, my primary concern was how information gleaned from this cohort of youth, maturing throughout the economically prosperous yet deficit-ridden and increasingly budget-driven 1980s and early 1990s, might inform contemporary policy debates about income inequality, poverty dynamics, and economic well-being. Many previously mentioned studies relied on the PSID, a nationally representative longitudinal survey of approximately 5,000 American families begun in 1968 (Duncan, 1984; McLanahan and Sandefur, 1994). Hence, those studies reflected poverty and income dynamics of a cohort of the general population, not just youth, growing older in a generation in which Liberal Democrats and their accompanying ideology of an activist role of government in society and the economy dominated political philosophy and discourse (Caputo, 1994). My use of the NLSY provides an opportunity to examine poverty and income dynamics in an era that witnessed the emergence and eventual ascendancy of a still-yet-to-be (if ever) fully realized political philosophy that promotes a diminished role for government in society and the economy and greater personal responsibility for one's economic well-being (Armey, 1995; Block, 1996; Gingrich, 1995). At issue in part was the extent to which ethnicity/race and sex still mattered in the economic well-being of families. Given the changing philosophy of social provision that occurred during this period and which found full expression in the Personal Responsibility and Work Opportunity Reconciliation Act of 1996 (that is, from dependence on government to assure income maintenance of economically disadvantaged groups to greater reliance on market mechanisms to promote self-sufficiency regardless of economic well-being), to what extent were maturing white youth in general and white males in particular able to position themselves within a family context to further their economic well-being more so than others? In short, did living in white families, particularly for males, still have its privileges? At issue also was the extent to which knowledge of different factors affecting the economic well-being of families stratified by sex and ethnicity/race might inform labor- and welfare-related policies and programs meant to prevent and/or buffer the adverse consequences of too low or too severe an erosion of economic well-being.

The present study contains three empirically-based chapters which include sections on measures, procedures, and results, as well as respective discussions of implications. A fourth chapter integrates the findings and discusses broader implications in light of policy and program options aimed to enhance economic well-being. Unlike Burtless (1995) who focused on wages, this study uses family income as the unit of analysis. I focus on family income rather than on individual wages per se because it more accurately reflects economic well-being over the span of respondents' lives, in part serving to moderate the extremes associated with changes in wage-related earnings (Duncan, Boisjoly, and Smeeding, 1997). Controlling for family size and its relation to poverty thresholds, I am able to assess how economic well-being, construed more broadly than individual wages, might change as the youth cohort matures into their prime working years, as they move from legally dependent status as youth to form their own families as adults. At issue is the extent to which economic well-being in more youthful years changes as the cohort matures. The extent of change can offer insight into background and other factors associated with the likelihood of escaping poverty or of becoming affluent, and, by extension, into the merits of arguments calling for primary prevention strategies focusing more exclusively on economic mobility than on tertiary responses focusing on insuring an economic floor to address issues of family poverty and income inequality (Kelso, 1994).

Chapter 1 continues by describing the level and distribution of income disparity found in the youth cohort between 1979 and 1993. Chapter 2 focuses on trends in and the relative influence of demographic, human capital, and psychological variables on economic well-being by sex and ethnicity/race between 1979 and 1993. Chapter 3 assesses the influence of demographic, human-capital, cumulative event, and psychological variables on the economic mobility among families of the youth cohort. The remainder of this chapter addresses the following questions in regard to the youth cohort aged 14 to 22 in

1979 as they matured throughout the 1980s and early 1990s:

1. What were the levels and trends of income disparity?
2. What were the levels and trends of affluence and poverty rates?
3. How did the levels and trends of income disparity and of poverty and affluence rates vary by sex and ethnicity/race?

Data and Measures

Data for the study were obtained from the National Longitudinal Survey of Youth (NLSY), a nationally representative sample of noninstitutionalized youth in the U.S. aged 14 to 22 in 1979 when first interviewed and annually surveyed thereafter. Documentation about the sample was found in the NLS Handbook 1995 (Center for Human Resource Research, 1995).

Poor respondents were those whose family income fell below the official poverty thresholds, which account for family size (Social Security Administration, 1995). Following Danziger and Gottschalk (1995), rich or affluent respondents were those whose family incomes exceeded seven times their respective poverty thresholds. Class of respondents refers to their status as either poor or affluent. In this chapter, I used two measures of income dispersion. The affluent-to-poor income ratio (INCRATIO) signified the level of income disparity between affluent and poor families, while the affluent-to-poor percentage share of the population ratio (POPRATIO) indicated the degree of dispersion between the rate of the population that lived in affluent families and that of those living in poor families.

The further either ratio was from the value of 1, the greater the respective disparity in income or in shares of the population between affluent and poor families. A POPRATIO equal to 1, for example, indicated that the rates of affluence and poverty were equal; less than 1, that the affluence rate was less than the poverty rate; and a POPRATIO greater than 1 indicated that it was greater than the poverty rate. A POPRATIO increasing over time signified growth in the affluent share of the population compared to the poverty share.

Respondents who reported $0.00 family income were assigned an annual nominal income of $1.00. Respondents for whom family income was reported as missing were assigned the mean value of family income respectively stratified by sex and ethnicity/race. Family income was adjusted for inflation using the Consumer Price Index for all items (CPI-U). It should also be noted that in the data files, income levels appeared to be capped at $75,000 prior to 1984 and at $100,000 in 1984 and afterward, with outliers assigned one value that differed from year to year. In any given year, the actual frequency of outliers was relatively small, ranging from a low of 16 or 0.5% of the study sample in 1984 to a high of 105 or 3.8% in 1993. The median was 35 or 1.3% of the study sample in 1983. Rather than delete the outliers from the study and to insure consistency by retaining them, I capped family income at $75,001 prior to 1984 and at $100,001 in 1984 and afterward, in effect slightly depressing the aggregate income of affluent families and thereby resulting in less income disparity than might have been the case otherwise. The caps, however, did not affect analyses in the remainder of this chapter that use median income, nor those in Chapter 3 that stratify the sample into deciles whose cutoff for the uppermost tier fell below the income caps every year.

Table 1.1 summarizes the variables used in this chapter.

Table 1.1 *Income Inequality Study Variables*

CLASS	Economic status, either affluent (>7 times the official poverty level) or poor
ETHNICITY/ RACE	Black, White, Hispanic (non-white, non-black)
INCRATIO	Affluent-to-poor income ratio: total income of affluent families/total income of poor families
POPRATIO	Affluent-to-poor percentage share of the population ratio: weighted percent of respondents living in affluent families/weighted percent of those in poor families
SEX	Female, male
TOTAL FAMILY INCOME	Income from all sources into the family unit
YEARS	1979-1993

Procedures

First, I show the mean and median total income of respondents living in affluent and poor families by year and sex and ethnicity/race. Second, the results of time series analysis using simple regression indicate the secular trend in median income adjusted for inflation for affluent and poor families by sex and ethnicity/race between 1979 and 1993. I report the Coefficient of Determination (r^2)

and the Durbin-Watson Statistic (*d*) for autocorrelation. In general, if *d* is close to 2, it is assumed that autocorrelation is not a problem. To the extent autocorrelation is problematic, the slope and strength of the coefficients are less reliable, as is the predictive ability of the regression model. Third, to determine if mean annual income differed among sex and ethnicity/race groups by class, the general linear model (GLM) procedure was conducted separately on affluent and poor families for each of the 15 study years. The GLM is used with unbalanced designs, that is, when cell sizes are unequal, as is the case among the sex and ethnicity/race groups used in this study. When appropriate for studentized-range post hoc analysis of mean annual income between pairs of the six sex and ethnicity/race groups, the least squared means (LSMEANS) procedure was used. The F ratio, follow-up pairwise comparisons, and results of their respective tests of statistical significance are reported (Cody & Smith, 1997).

Fourth, I then show the affluent-to-poor income ratio (INCRATIO), 1979-1993, by sex and ethnicity/race and report results of time series analyses to determine the level and direction of trends in income disparity. Fifth, I show the percent shares of the population living in affluent or poor families and the trends in the rates of poverty and affluence stratified by sex and ethnicity/race. Finally, I present the affluent-to-poor percent share of the population ratio (POPRATIO) by year, ethnicity/race, and sex.

Results

The study sample (N=2,745), which included respondents about whom all relevant information as noted above was available, differed slightly from the original population sample (N=12,686) on three socio-demographic measures in 1979: age (18.89 years old compared to 17.89), total net family income ($17,144 compared to $14,706), and proportion of black respondents (31% compared to 24.9%). On a fourth such measure, family size, the study and population samples were comparable (4.49 compared to 4.46). Given these differences on three of four measures, generalizability is somewhat compromised and the results and discussions in this and subsequent chapters are presented with this limitation in mind.

Levels and Trends of Income Disparity. Table 1.2 shows the mean and median total income of respondents living in affluent and poor families by year, while Table 1.3 shows the respective percent increases, Coefficients of Determination, and the Durbin-Watson Statistics of median total income between 1979 and 1993, by sex and ethnicity/race.

Table 1.2 *Mean and (Median) Total Income[1] of Affluent and Poor Families, 1979-1993, by Sex and Ethnicity/Race*

			Male						Female					
	Total		Black		White		Hispanic		Black		White		Hispanic	
Year	Rich	Poor	Rich	Poor	Rich	Poor	Rich	Poor	Rich	Poor	Rich	Poor	Rich	Poor
1979	38429	3443	37497	3698	39198	3071	49731[2]	3935	36171	3924	38223	2622	34200	3144
()	36300	2933	36300	3056	39603	3049	49731[2]	3993	29040	3296	36300	2613	34485	2904
1980	44894	4038	38153[2]	5161	47053	3132	42704	5098	43592	4275	44508	3093	37327[2]	4284
()	44496	3669	32960[2]	4611	45320	2711	40499	4944	41200	3829	4496	2872	39552[2]	4522
1981	52515	5299	45371	6370	53817	5564	53237[2]	5563	57407	5346	49006	4110	55799	5223
()	53631	4999	43745	5736	59085	5454	63630[2]	5635	64050	4892	49995	4526	54925	4936
1982	53688	6153	49495[2]	6637	53659	4949	64751[2]	7683	55464[2]	6699	54735	5183	47108	5971
()	53075	5625	38600[2]	5790	53075	4848	64751[2]	6147	45355[2]	5772	54040	5314	45452	5790
1983	57521	6358	51169[2]	6392	57367	5474	55706	8221	63527[2]	6821	58009	5121	53025[2]	6827
()	59262	5754	51169[2]	5819	59760	4980	45246	7105	69720[2]	5976	59760	4980	55776[2]	5868
1984	68333	6747	59920	7159	68269	6038	73571[2]	6729	61152	6976	71223	6034	61277	7505
()	62340	6234	56106	6275	62340	5764	67535[2]	6263	48386	6246	67535	6175	55274	7686
1985	71600	6823	67872	6996	67905	5594	75275	7999	77963	7207	73702	6249	73023	6983
()	68864	6518	69940	5796	65227	4466	75521	8070	75320	6791	70244	6456	72092	6681
1986	73632	7043	67587	4885	71171	5605	81442	7885	88052	7811	75046	7099	69527	7562
()	67930	6760	64850	3143	66088	5101	73377	8384	99301	7120	70144	7069	61841	7075

Table 1.2 *Mean and (Median) Total Income[1] of Affluent and Poor Families, 1979-1993, by Sex and Ethnicity/Race continued*

1987	78404	7220	63661	5698	74981	6050	80787	7709	71136	7804	83899	7270	78415	7288
()	78120	7077	62025	5143	73840	5680	76112	7238	66680	7163	85995	7783	80656	7238
1988	91196	7875	86572	6807	87401	8240	81216	11656	92504	7749	94559	7282	99934	8929
()	89553	7930	83519	6576	87281	9464	78078	11830	89286	7878	93989	7850	93634	8782
1989	95893	8799	86730	6258	95601	8817	98875	8888	87005	9061	97673	8128	104573	11468
()	94494	9039	84386	5580	94550	8680	98332	10788	86800	9329	95945	8804	124000	12786
1990	104635	8950	97200	6297	105613	10326	108199	7016	93483	9231	104626	9005	112487	10816
()	105344	9314	100508	4077	105474	10456	111944	3921	97763	9473	104821	9828	122989	11763
1991	112669	9610	102576	6878	114605	9100	110267	10188	104783	10094	113918	9645	110071	11748
()	111956	9926	102150	5815	116178	9051	119787	12721	107870	10386	113863	9185	111888	13282
1992	116773	10523	104273	6580	118651	10030	110829	13531	93838	10934	119953	11540	124204	12518
()	120026	10330	112415	4910	125568	9821	110994	18239	96880	10471	121219	11224	137494	12921
1993	121501	11732	118054	8505	122230	9523	128226	22545	121048	11798	121183	12416	118273	12674
()	126334	11913	118663	7297	130339	8019	136552	23409	118490	11969	122102	12419	119213	15185

[1] Dollars adjusted for inflation using the CPI-U, All Items.

[2] $n \leq 5$.

Table 1.3 *Percent Increase, Coefficients, and Durbin-Watson Statistic for Median Total Income of Affluent and Poor Families, 1979-1993, by Sex and Ethnicity/Race*

Statistics	Total		Male						Female					
			Black		White		Hispanic		Black		White		Hispanic	
	Rich	Poor	Rich	Poor	Rich	Poor	Rich	Poor	Rich	Poor	Rich	Poor	Rich	Poor
% Increase														
	248	266	216	97	232	161	174	484	227	205	219	373	248	382
b	6262	585	6212	87	6337	491	5926	911	5717	559	6287	629	7377	805
T	22.38[a]	5.06[a]	5.98[a]	1.24	14.08[a]	6.44[a]	10.27[a]	4.30[a]	7.63[a]	21.99[a]	31.48[a]	19.90[a]	10.77[a]	12.02[a]
r^2	.97	.97	.95	.11	.93	.76	.89	.58	.82	.97	.98	.97	.90	.92
d	0.66	1.01	1.78	1.67	0.50	1.58	1.59	1.17	3.08	1.32	1.54	1.95	1.71	1.50

Note: Percent increase reflects the difference between median family income in 1979 and 1993. For the Durbin-Watson Statistic, with the number of independent variables k = 1 and n = 15, the critical values for comparing *d* at the .05 level of statistical significance are such that there is evidence of positive autocorrelation when $d < .81$ and of negative autocorrelation when $d > 3.19$.

[a] $p < .001$

Controlling for inflation, between 1979 and 1993 median family income increased for respondents living in affluent and poor families. In 1979, affluent families had a median income of $36,300 compared to $126,334 in 1993, while the median income of poor families increased from $2,933 to $11,913. The strength and magnitude of the trends were significant for both affluent and poor families. Each year was likely to result in a $6,262 increase for affluent families and $585 for poor families. The strength and magnitude of these overall trends, however, varied by sex and ethnicity/race. As Table 1.3 shows, among poor families, those of Hispanic men had the greatest increase in median income when 1979 was compared to 1993, 484%, as well as the largest likely annual increase, $911, between 1979 and 1993. Time, however, accounted for only 58% of the variance in median income, signifying a modest upward trend throughout the study period. By contrast, median income for poor white women increased by 373% when 1979 was compared to 1993 and it was likely to increase annually by $629. Time, however, accounted for 97% of the variance in median income, signifying a strongly positive trend between 1979 and 1993. Families of poor black males experienced the most gradual increase in median income, 97%, when 1979 was compared to 1993, and on average about $87 per year. Regardless of sex and ethnicity/race among affluent families, median income increased steeply between 1979 and 1993.

Table 1.4 shows the GLM results of within-class differences in mean income of affluent and poor families between 1979 and 1993, by sex and ethnicity/race.

Table 1.4 *GLM Results of Differences in Mean Income of Affluent and Poor Families, 1979-1993*

Year	Affluent	F	n	Poor	F	n
1979	HM,WM,WF,BM,BF,HF	0.70	126	HM, BF, BM, HF, WM, WF; HM>WF[b]; BF>HF[a]; BF>WM[c]; BF>WF[a]; BM>WF[b]	4.97[a]	506
1980	WM,WF,BF,HM,BM,HF	0.99	110	BM,HM,HF,BF>WM[b]; BM>BF[c];BM>WF[a]; HM>WF[b]; BF>WF[a]	7.96[a]	502
1981	BF,HF,WM,HM,WF,BM	0.88	129	BM,WM,HM,BF,HF>WF[c]; BM>BF[c]; BM>HF[c]; BM>WF[a]; WM>WF[b]; BF>WF[b]	4.73[a]	495
1982	HM,BF,WF,WM,BM,HF	0.64	79	HM,BF,BM,HF,WF,WM; HM>WF[b]; HM>WM[b]; BF>WF[a]; BF>WM[b]; BM>WF[b]; BM>WM[b]	4.64[a]	538
1983	BF,WF,WM,HM,HF,BM	0.34	96	HM,HF,BF,BM,WM,WF; HM>BM[c]; HM>WM[b]; HM>WF[a]; HF>WF[c]; BF>WM[c]; BF>WF[a]; BM>WF[c]	4.66[a]	525
1984	HF,WF,WM,HF,BF,BM	0.72	129	HF,BM,BF,HM,WM,WF	1.40	470
1985	BF,HM,WF,HF,WM,BM	0.75	153	HM,BF,BM,HF,WF,WM	1.76	432
1986	BF,HM,WF,WM,HF,BM	1.38	169	HM,BF,HF,WF,WM,BM; HM>WM[c]; HM>BM[b]; BF>WM[b]; BF>BM[a]; HF>WM[c]; HF>BM[b]; WF>BM[b]	4.76[a]	430

Table 1.4 *GLM Results of Differences in Mean Income of Affluent and Poor Families, 1979-1993 continued*

Year	Affluent	F	n	Poor	F	n
1987	WF,HM,HF,WM,BF,BM; WF>WM[b]; WF>BM[a]	2.61[c]	203	BF,HM,HF,WF,WM,BM	1.99	384
1988	HF,WF,BF,WM,BM,HM	1.51	198	HM,HF,WM,BF,WF,BM; HM>WM[c]; HM>BF[b]; HM>WF[b]; HM>BM[a]; HF>BM[c]	3.05[c]	340
1989	HF,HM,WF,WM,BF,BM	1.40	224	HF>BF[c],HM,WM,WF,BM; HF>HM[c]; HF>WM[c]; HF>WF[b]; HF>BM[a]; BF>BM[b]; WF>BM[c]	4.14[b]	342
1990	HF,HM,WM,WF,BM,BF	1.31	218	HF,WM,BF,WF,HM,BM; HF>HM[c]; HF>BM[a]; WM>BM[b]; BF>BM[b]; WF>BM[b]	3.83[b]	362
1991	WM,WF,HM,HF,BF,BM	1.12	209	HF,HM,BF,WF,WM,BM; HF>BM[a]; BF>BM[a]; WF>BM[c]	3.33[b]	330
1992	HF,WF,WM,HM,BM,BF; HF>BF[b]; WF>BM[c]; WF>BF[b]; WM>BM[b]; WM>BF[b]	3.28[b]	207	HM,HF,WF,BF,WM>BM[c]; HM>BM[a]; HM>BM[a]; WF>BM[a]; BF>BM[a]	5.91[a]	350
1993	HM,WM,WF,BF,HF,BM	0.25	158	HM>HF[c], WF, BF, WM, BM; HF>BM[c]; WF>BM[b]; BF>BM[c]	7.08[a]	288

Legend: BM = Black Male, WM = White Male, HM = Hispanic Male, BF = Black Female, WF = White Female, HF = Hispanic Female [a] $p < .001$; [b] $p < .01$; [c] $p < .05$

Differences in income among affluent families were found only in 1987, when white females had greater total average income than white men and black men, and in 1992, when Hispanic females had greater income than black females and when white females and males had greater income than black males and females. As noted earlier, the capping of incomes may have flattened the distribution more than might had been the case otherwise, thereby minimizing differences by sex and ethnicity/race. A separate analysis revealed that outliers were assigned one value that varied by year, but not by sex and ethnicity/race. Nonetheless, the distribution of income among outliers was roughly similar to the study sample stratified by sex and ethnicity/race, thereby casting some doubt on the prospect that the reason so few differences were found among affluent families stratified by sex and ethnicity/race was an artifact of capping income. Hence, the GLM results in all likelihood are as accurate a depiction of income disparity among affluent families stratified by sex and ethnicity/race as can be determined given the limitations of the NLSY data files. There was much more income disparity among poor families than among affluent families, particularly during the early and later years of the study period. Between 1979 and 1983, as the country experienced a transition from stagflation to recession, in general poor black and Hispanic families had higher levels of total income than did poor white families. Between 1988 and 1993, however, Hispanic families still fared well compared to others, but particularly so compared to those of black men.

Table 1.5 shows the affluent-to-poor income ratio (INCRATIO), 1979-1993, by sex and ethnicity/race, while Table 1.6 shows the respective INCRATIO percent changes, Coefficients of Determination, and the Durbin-Watson Statistics.

Table 1.5: *Affluent-to-Poor Income Ratio, 1979-1993, by Sex and Ethnicity/Race*

		Male			Female		
Year	Total	Black	White	Hispanic	Black	White	Hispanic
1979	11.16	10.13	12.76	12.63	9.21	14.57	10.87
1980	11.11	7.39	15.02	8.37	10.19	14.38	8.71
1981	9.91	7.12	9.67	9.56	10.73	12.43	10.68
1982	8.72	7.45	10.84	8.42	8.27	10.56	7.88
1983	9.04	8.00	10.47	6.77	9.31	11.32	7.76
1984	10.12	8.36	11.30	10.93	8.76	11.80	8.16
1985	10.49	9.70	12.13	9.41	10.81	11.79	10.45
1986	10.45	13.83	12.69	10.32	11.27	10.57	9.19
1987	10.85	11.17	12.39	10.47	9.11	11.54	10.75
1988	11.58	12.71	10.60	6.96	11.93	12.98	11.19
1989	10.89	13.85	10.84	11.12	9.60	12.01	9.11
1990	11.69	15.43	10.22	15.42	10.12	11.61	10.40
1991	11.72	14.91	12.59	10.82	10.38	11.81	9.36
1992	11.09	15.84	11.82	8.19	8.58	10.39	9.92
1993	10.35	13.88	12.83	5.68	10.26	9.76	9.33

Table 1.6 *Percent Change, Coefficients, and Durbin-Watson Statistic for the Affluent-to-Poor Income Ratio, 1979-1993, by Sex and Ethnicity/Race*

		Male			Female		
Statistics	Total	Black	White	Hispanic	Black	White	Hispanic
% Change	-7	37	1	-55	11	-33	-14
b	0.086	0.626	-0.023	-0.03	0.0316	-0.187	0.037
T	1.71	6.55[a]	-0.278	-0.217	0.49	-2.83[b]	0.535
r^2	0.18	.77	.01	.00	.02	.38	.02
d	0.80	1.38	1.82	1.49	2.50	0.94	1.94

Note: Percent change reflects the difference between mean family income in 1979 and 1993. For the Durbin-Watson Statistic, with the number of independent variables k = 1 and n = 15, the critical values for comparing *d* at the .05 level of statistical significance are such that there is evidence of positive autocorrelation when $d < .81$ and of negative autocorrelation when $d > 3.19$.

[a] $p < .001$; [b] $p < .05$

Despite the 7% drop between the affluent-to-poor income ratio (INCRATIO) in 1993 from that in 1979 for the entire sample, the secular trend was positive, though weak and not statistically significant. Significant trends were found for two of the six groups, black men and white women. Income disparity increased by 37% between 1979 and 1993 for black men and the secular trend was strongly positive. For white women, income disparity declined by 33% between 1979 and 1993, while the secular trend was more modest than that of black men. Though not statistically significant, income disparity decreased between affluent and poor families of Hispanic males and females, while it increased for white males and black women.

Overall, results showed that income increased to a statistically significant degree for affluent and poor families for most men and women regardless of ethnicity/race. The major exception was for black men, whose family income increased modestly, but not to a statistically significant degree, between 1979 and 1993. Due to the substantial increase in income of affluent families and the modest increase for poor families, income disparity increased for black men. The families of poor black men lost ground compared to those of affluent black men. Despite increases in income among affluent and poor families, income disparity declined for white women. The families of poor white women gained relative to those of affluent white women. These findings suggest that many in the youth cohort became increasingly better off economically as they matured in a roughly equitable manner. Poor white women made the greatest relative gains, while poor black men gained the least when contrasted to their affluent counterparts.

Levels and Trends in the Rates of Poverty and Affluence. Table 1.7 shows the weighted distribution, or percent share of the population, living in affluent or poor families, 1979-1993, by sex and ethnicity/race, while Table 1.8 shows the changes in the poverty and affluence rates in 1979 from those in 1993, as well as results of time series analysis, that is, the Coefficients of Determination, and the Durbin-Watson Statistic, of the affluence and poverty rates, 1979-1993.

Table 1.7 *Percent [1] of Affluent and Poor Families, 1979-1993, by Sex and Ethnicity/Race*

			Male						Female					
	Total		Black		White		Hispanic		Black		White		Hispanic	
Year	Rich	Poor	Rich	Poor	Rich	Poor	Rich	Poor	Rich	Poor	Rich	Poor	Rich	Poor
1979	6.3	12.9	2.3	25.8	9.0	8.5	1.0	15.7	2.4	32.3	5.8	10.1	5.1	22.2
1980	5.7	12.9	1.4	21.6	8.4	9.0	2.0	10.8	2.1	33.3	5.2	10.2	2.1	22.3
1981	6.8	12.6	2.8	22.1	9.5	9.3	2.7	11.4	1.2	33.4	6.5	9.2	2.2	21.3
1982	3.9	13.6	1.2	24.1	5.3	8.3	0.8	13.0	1.1	38.9	3.8	10.7	2.3	24.1
1983	4.9	12.9	0.1	17.9	7.5	7.8	3.0	15.0	1.1	40.1	4.5	10.3	1.9	21.3
1984	6.5	11.9	1.8	23.1	9.1	6.4	5.2	10.0	1.4	33.9	6.3	10.2	3.5	21.0
1985	6.9	10.7	3.9	16.1	8.5	5.8	7.6	13.0	2.8	32.2	6.9	9.2	4.6	17.2
1986	8.2	10.3	3.9	17.5	10.8	4.9	8.7	13.4	1.6	31.4	8.1	8.8	4.0	21.2
1987	9.8	9.1	3.3	17.6	11.6	3.3	8.9	6.6	2.6	31.4	11.0	7.6	3.7	22.7
1988	9.2	7.7	3.3	14.2	10.0	3.0	4.7	7.5	3.8	27.6	11.2	5.8	3.2	20.8
1989	10.7	8.2	4.7	12.2	13.8	3.7	7.2	10.4	3.2	26.0	10.9	7.2	4.7	18.2
1990	10.6	8.5	5.3	15.5	13.5	3.6	6.8	7.8	2.2	29.8	11.0	6.8	4.4	18.5
1991	9.9	7.9	5.4	16.5	12.1	3.0	5.8	6.9	1.0	26.8	10.8	7.0	5.1	13.6
1992	9.9	8.7	5.7	18.3	13.8	2.6	10.1	6.9	1.6	26.4	9.0	9.1	4.1	13.9
1993	7.4	7.3	5.1	12.5	10.0	3.4	7.8	5.2	2.4	23.3	6.5	6.8	2.8	11.3

[1] Weighted for each year.

Table 1.8 *Percent Change, Coefficients, and Durbin-Watson Statistic for Rates of Affluence and Poverty, 1979-1993, by Sex and Ethnicity/Race*

			Male						Female					
	Total		Black		White		Hispanic		Black		White		Hispanic	
Year	Rich	Poor	Rich	Poor	Rich	Poor	Rich	Poor	Rich	Poor	Rich	Poor	Rich	Poor
% Change	17	-43	121	-52	11	-60	680	-66	0	-27	12	-32	-51	-49
b	0.360	-0.472	0.325	-0.745	0.389	-0.521	0.530	-0.590	0.040	-0.819	0.396	-0.27	0.0917	-0.685
T	4.054[b]	-9.155[a]	5.604[a]	-4.806[a]	3.670[b]	-9.502[a]	4.628[a]	-4.756[a]	0.789	-4.593[a]	3.314[b]	-4.244[b]	1.430	-4.965[a]
r^2	.56	.86	0.71	0.64	0.51	0.87	0.62	0.64	0.05	0.62	0.49	0.58	0.14	0.65
d	0.99	0.90	1.36	2.18	1.73	0.69	1.41	2.20	1.12	1.03	0.66	1.37	1.31	1.19

Note: Percent change reflects the respective differences between the rates of affluence and poverty in 1979 and 1993. For the Durbin-Watson Statistic, with the number of independent variables k = 1 and n = 15, the critical values for comparing *d* at the .05 level of statistical significance are such that there is evidence of positive autocorrelation when $d < .81$ and of negative autocorrelation when $d > 3.19$.

[a] $p < .001$; [b] $p < .01$

In 1979, 6.3% of families were affluent, while more than twice that (12.9%) were poor. In 1993, the percentage of affluent families increased by 17%, to 7.4% of the youth cohort, while that of poor families declined by 43%, to 7.3%. Although a modestly increasing proportion of all families became affluent between 1979 and 1993, there was a decline after 1989. And although the proportion of poor families decreased strongly between 1979 and 1993, after 1988 the direction of the trend was less clear. Significantly modest increases in the proportion of families becoming affluent were found only for males, while significantly modest decreases in the proportion of poor families were found for all groups except white males. Although the proportion of poor white families of male respondents also declined from 8.5% in 1979 to 3.4% in 1993, autocorrelation was found in the secular trend, thereby confounding the result.

Table 1.9 shows the ratio of the rates of affluent-to-poor families (POPRATIO), 1979-1993, by sex and ethnicity/race.

Table 1.9 *Ratio of the Rates of Affluence and Poverty, 1979-1993, by Sex and Ethnicity/Race*

			Male			Female	
Year	Total	Black	White	Hispanic	Black	White	Hispanic
1979	0.49	0.09	1.06	0.06	0.07	0.57	0.22
1980	0.44	0.06	0.93	0.19	0.06	0.51	0.09
1981	0.53	0.12	1.02	0.23	0.03	0.71	0.10
1982	0.29	0.05	0.64	0.06	0.03	0.36	0.10
1983	0.38	0.01	0.96	0.20	0.03	0.44	0.09
1984	0.55	0.08	1.42	0.52	0.0	0.61	0.16
1985	0.64	0.24	1.47	0.58	0.09	0.75	0.27
1986	0.80	0.22	2.20	0.64	0.05	0.92	0.19
1987	1.07	0.19	3.52	1.35	0.08	1.45	0.16
1988	1.19	0.23	3.33	0.63	0.14	1.93	0.15
1989	1.30	0.39	3.73	0.69	0.12	1.51	0.26
1990	1.25	0.34	3.75	0.87	0.07	1.62	0.24
1991	1.25	0.33	4.03	0.84	0.04	1.54	0.38
1992	1.14	0.31	5.31	1.46	0.06	0.99	0.29
1993	1.01	0.41	2.94	1.50	0.10	0.96	0.25

In 1979 the proportion of the cohort living in affluent families was about half (49%) that of those in poor families and by 1993 roughly equivalent proportions lived in either affluent (7.4%) or poor (7.3%) families (POPRATIO = 1.01). This aggregate equalization, however, masked differences by sex and ethnicity/race. The proportion of black men living in affluent and poor families became increasingly equal, but the POPRATIO remained below .50 throughout the entire period. The proportion of white men living in either affluent (9.0%) or poor (8.5%) families was nearly equal in 1979, but by the early 1990s, white men were more than 2 to 5 times as likely to live in affluent families than in poor families. Hispanic males were far more likely to live in poor families in the early 1980s, with POPRATIOs exceeding .50 only after 1983. Greater proportions of Hispanic men lived in affluent than poor families only in 1987, 1992, and 1993.

Black women, like black men, were far more likely to live in poor than affluent families between 1979 and 1993. The POPRATIO for black women peaked at .14 in 1988, signifying that they made the least movement toward a more proportionate distribution of the cohort between affluent and poor families. Like black women, Hispanic women were more likely to live in poor than affluent families between 1979 and 1993, but at a slightly higher degree of equalization. The POPRATIO for Hispanic women peaked at .38 in 1991. The proportion of white women in affluent families varied considerably in the early 1980s, but many more were nonetheless likely to live in poor rather than affluent families. Between 1987 and 1991, however, white women were one and one-half to two times more likely to live in affluent than poor families, and they were equally as likely to reside in either in 1992 and 1993.

Discussion

Much has been written about the increasing disparity between higher and lower income Americans in the 1980s and 1990s (Bartlett and Steele, 1992; Blank, 1997; Bok, 1994; Caputo, 1995b; Danziger and Gottschalk, 1993 and 1995; Hacker, 1992; Kozol, 1991; Reich, 1997). At the nationally broadcasted, pre-inaugural Clinton-Gore Economic Conference in Little Rock, Arkansas, economists Robert Solow and Alan Blinder cited increasing inequality as a major economic problem facing the nation, a theme echoed during the second Clinton administration by self-proclaimed "Progressive Democrats" such as pollster Stanley B. Greenberg and Harvard University professor of government and sociology Theda Skocpol (Economic Conference, 1992; Greenberg and Skocpol, 1997a). According to much commentary in the popular press and inference from the more scholarly work, in general throughout the Reagan-Bush years and continuing into the Clinton presidency, the rich got richer and the poor got poorer for much of the population.

Results thus far of this study, which focused on a youth cohort entering their primary family formation and work years during this period, suggested that this subset of the population went against the grain in at least one important aspect. Both affluent and poor families were better off economically. Median income of both poor and affluent families increased for all groups within the youth cohort, albeit at different rates. Maturing women and Hispanic males living in poor families saw their income levels rise more than others, while the family income of black males rose least. Affluent families experienced more equitable (perhaps due in part to capping) income by sex or ethnicity/race and generally steeper increases in median income. Thus, the aphorism that the rich got richer and the poor poorer would be a somewhat inaccurate characterization of this cohort as they matured throughout the 1980s and early 1990s. Despite the income gap, the rich got richer, but the poor were also better off. Affluent families, however, were more uniformly better off, having strongly positive gains in total income between 1979 and 1993. On the whole, with the exceptions 1987 and 1992, affluent families demonstrated virtually no income disparity regardless of sex and ethnicity/race. Poor families, on the other hand, differentially experienced increased income, with men in general and black men in particular having more modest rising increases in family income between 1979 and 1993 than women. On the whole, with the exception of 1985, poor families exhibited varying degrees of income disparity, reflecting the differential increases in total income throughout the study period.

In regard to another aspect of income disparity, namely the gap which separated the affluent from the poor despite increases in median income for both groups, other findings of this study corroborated much of the previously cited popular commentary and scholarly work. For the entire cohort, income disparity between affluent and poor families increased, albeit somewhat less sharply than reported for the population as a whole. This aggregate finding, however, masked significant variation in magnitude and direction within the cohort stratified by sex and ethnicity/race. Given the weakest trend increase in family income, income disparity increased sharply for black males. For white women, however, income disparity decreased. Given the high probability of ethnicity/race homogeneity within families, this finding should come as no surprise. By extension, as the cohort matured and formed their own family units, white women would be more likely to position themselves with white men, who were shown to live in families that were economically better off than all others in every study year, while black men would be more likely to position themselves with black women, who were shown to be the worst off economically in many of the study years. For the remaining groups, the trend in income disparity between affluent and poor families decreased, but not to a statistically significant degree. Nonetheless such a finding suggests that income disparity between affluent and poor families might have been less for families of the youthful cohort maturing throughout the 1980s and early 1990s than for the general working-age population as a whole.

In regard to changes in the distribution of respondents who lived in poor and rich families between 1979 and 1993, findings of this study in general corroborated those of Danziger and Gottschalk (1995), Blank (1997), and Caputo (1998), although there were some differences when accounting for sex and ethnicity/race. Essentially, as the economy expanded throughout the 1980s, poverty rates declined for most groups. The trend for white males could not be reliably determined due to autocorrelation. Reflecting relatively high starting positions, the poverty rates of black women and men had the steepest declines over the study period, followed by Hispanic women and men, and white women. Despite an economy that experienced its second longest and strongest economic expansion between 1983 and 1989, these declines were quite modest. The expanding economy nonetheless enabled affluence rates of males to increase. Having the lowest affluence rate at the start of the study period, Hispanic men had the steepest upward trend between 1979 and 1993. White males, who began with the highest affluence rate, had the second steepest upward trend.

By the end of the study period, the poverty and affluence rates had become more equal in the aggregate. There were more affluent families and fewer poor families, again signifying the general improvement of economic conditions. But equalization rates varied considerably by sex and ethnicity/race, in part reflecting relative starting positions in 1979 and in turn mirroring differential gains in rates of affluent families and declines in rates of poor families. Black men and women were more likely than other groups, with the exception of Hispanic men, to live in poverty in 1979 and, despite increases in the numbers of affluent families, they were still more likely to do so in 1993. White males had started out much more evenly distributed between affluent and poor families in 1979, but by 1993 they were much more likely to be living in affluent families; whereas white women were more likely to have started out in poor families, but toward the end of the study period, to a lesser degree than white males, they were also more likely to reside in affluent families. On the whole, being white still had its privileges, and being white and male had even more.

Chapter 2
ECONOMIC WELL-BEING

Introduction

Having assessed the nature and extent of income inequality and shares of the study sample living in affluent compared to poor families, the focus now shifts to the economic well-being of the youth cohort as a whole. This chapter describes the levels of and trends in economic well-being among all families of the study sample, in the aggregate and stratified by sex and ethnicity/race, for whom all requisite information was available. Likewise, it assesses the influence of demographic, human capital, and psychological variables on economic well-being. The chapter seeks to shed insight on how well this national sample of maturing respondents fared throughout the 1980s and early 1990s. As noted previously, researchers primarily focusing on the adult population, which included those maturing in the late 1960s and throughout the 1970s, demonstrated that labor-market conditions, demographic factors, family structure, and ethnicity/race affected both income inequality and economic well-being and that psychological and personality-related attributes of individuals had little if any effect (Blank, 1997; Dolinsky, Caputo, and O'Kane, 1989; Duncan 1984; Danziger and Gottschalk, 1993 and 1995; Gottschalk, McLanahan, and Sandefur, 1994; Karoly, 1993; Levy and Michel, 1991). In an earlier related study of two sub-samples of the youth cohort used for present purposes, I found that psychological attributes such as self-esteem were moderately correlated with economic well-being in 1985 and 1992, but that, as with findings of related studies, socio-demographic factors including education, marital status, and ethnicity/race were far stronger predictors (Caputo, 1998). Likewise in two other studies using the same cohort, I found socio-demographic factors to be far stronger correlates of poverty dynamics than psychological attributes (Caputo, 1997 and 1999).

This chapter extends my earlier work using this youth cohort in several ways. First, it includes all 1994 respondents for whom requisite information was available in each survey year since 1979. Inclusion of all such respondents avoids limitations associated with trend comparisons based on different sub-samples of the cohort. Second, as in Chapter 1, this chapter takes advantage of the longitudinal nature of the NLSY data files and uses time-series analysis to examine trends in economic well-being in the youth cohort stratified by sex and ethnicity/race. As noted previously, because of its ability to detect autocorrelation, time-series analysis allows for a more accurate reflection of trends than do other time dimension portraits often presented in cross-sectional, cohort, and panel studies (Rubin and Babbie, 1997; Webster, 1992). And third, in regard to demographic, human capital, and psychological correlates of economic well-being, this chapter presents findings from three survey years, 1980, 1987, and 1993. It thereby provides three snapshots of the same correlates of economic well-being, some of which respectively include change variables, such as change in family size, from the previous survey years of 1979, 1986, and 1992, at the beginning, middle, and end of the study period. These snapshots enable an assessment of how these correlates of well-being varied as the cohort matured and formed their own families throughout the 1980s and early 1990s. With these snapshots, this chapter sheds light on how durable earlier, increasingly distal, parental factors were on the economic well-being of the cohort in later years when in their own family units. Chapter 2 addresses the following questions in regard to the youth cohort as it matured throughout the 1980s and early 1990s:

1. What were the levels and trends of economic well-being?
2. How did the levels and trends of economic well-being vary by sex and ethnicity/race?
3. What human capital, demographic, and psychological characteristics were correlated with economic well-being in selected years?
4. How did significant correlates of economic well-being vary by sex and ethnicity/race?

Measures

Following Danziger and Gottschalk (1995), I used the income-to-poverty ratio (IPR) as a general measure of economic well-being. IPR is the ratio of family income to the appropriate poverty threshold (Social Security Administration, 1995). A ratio below 1.00 signified that the income for families of a given size fell below the official definition of poverty, while a ratio of 1.00 or higher indicated income at or above the poverty level. A ratio of 2.75, for example, indicated that family income was 175% above the appropriate poverty threshold. As was the case in Chapter 1, respondents who reported $0.00 family income were assigned an annual nominal income of $1.00. Respondents for whom family income was reported as missing were assigned the mean value of family income respectively stratified by sex and ethnicity/race.

Table 2.1 summarizes the variables used in this chapter. The descriptive variables include ethnicity/race, the income-to-poverty ratio (IPR), and sex.

Table 2.1 *Descriptors and Correlates of Economic Well-Being*

DESCRIPTORS:	
ETHNICITY/RACE	Black, White, Hispanic (non-white, non-black)
IPR	Income-to-poverty ratio, i.e., the ratio of family income to the appropriate poverty threshold
SEX	Female, Male
CORRELATES:	
BACKGROUND VARIABLES:	
AGE R	Age of respondent
HGC R	Highest grade completed, respondent
HGC RM	Highest grade completed, respondent's mother
HOWK	Hours worked during the year
MS	Marital status (1 = married)
R SMSA	Residence within a Standard Metropolitan Statistical Area (1 = yes)
UNEMP R	Unemployment rate in area of residence
CHANGE VARIABLES:	
CFS	Change in family size from the preceding year
CHWK	Change in number of hours worked from the preceding year
PSYCHOLOGICAL VARIABLES:	
LOC	Rotter locus-of-control scale scores
SELF EST	Scores from the Rosenberg self-esteem scale

Correlates of economic well-being comprised background, change, and psychological variables. Background variables incorporated human capital and socio-demogrpahic characteristics of the respondent as an individual, of the respondent's family, and of the area in which the respondent lived. Human capital variables of age (AGE R), highest grade completed (HGC R), and hours worked (HOWK) referred to the respondent as an individual. Given findings of previous studies, each of these variables was expected to be positively associated with economic well-being. In addition, over time, the strength of their relation to economic well-being was expected to increase.

The background variable highest grade completed, respondent's mother (HGC RM) was used as a proxy for early human capital and other influences of respondents' parents on economic well-being. Given that most of the youth cohort lived in their parents' households in 1979 at the time of the first interview, the correlation of HGC RM was expected to lessen over time as respondents increasingly formed their own families and moved into their own households. Preliminary analyses helped rule out other early influential factors that may have also served as a proxy for early human capital and other influences of respondents' parents on economic well-being. For the entire study sample, for example, HGC RM was highly correlated with the highest grade completed of respondents' fathers (r = .63, p = .001). Both HGC RM and highest grade completed of respondents' fathers were each moderately correlated with the income-to-poverty ratio (IPR) in 1980 (r = .26 and .26 respectively, p = .001), 1987 (r = .26 and .29 respectively, p = .001), and 1993 (r = .24 and .28 respectively, p = .001). Of the two, however, the correlation coefficient (r) of HGC RM and HGC R, the highest grade completed by the respondent, was less than the .40 cutoff used to minimize the effects of multicolinearity among the correlates in each selected year: 1980 ($r = .37$, $p = .001$), 1987 ($r = .39$, $p = .001$), and 1993 ($r = .38$, $p = .001$). Hence, the mother's educational level rather than the father's was retained as the more appropriate proxy for early background correlates of a respondent's economic well-being.

Two background variables were meant to capture the larger environment in which respondents resided. The unemployment rate in area of residence (UNEMPR) was used as a measure of structural factors influencing economic well-being. To the extent that labor market conditions reflected opportunity for work, UNEMPR was expected to be inversely related to economic well-being, that is, higher rates of unemployment in the area of residence of the respondent signified lower levels of economic well-being (Blank, 1997). The other environmental or contextual variable, Residence within a Standard Metropolitan Statistical Area (R SMSA), coded 1 = yes, 0 = no, accounted for regional variation separating smaller, rural-based communities from larger, more urban-based ones. Given the extremes of affluence and poverty often found in larger urban areas and the productive capacity and lower per capita income often associated with more rural regions of the country, R SMSA was expected to have a weak positive correlation with economic well-being in the aggregate, but negative in the case of black families since disproportionately high concentrations of poor black families live in urban areas (Wilson, 1996).

The final background variable used in this chapter was marital status (MS), coded as 1 = married, 0 = not married. Given the findings of pervious research, MS was also expected to have little if no correlation with economic well-being in the early years of the study when most respondents were likely to be living in their parents' households, but to be positively associated with economic well-being as respondents matured. Given the youthfulness of the cohort over the duration of the study period, respondents forming their own households were likely to reside in dual-earner families upon marriage, and hence, have greater economic well-being when accounting for family size.

Previous research suggested that changes in marital status and labor force participation affected economic well-being. Hence, two related change variables were also used as correlates of economic well-being. Change in family size (CFS) was used to capture the effects of changes in family composition, which may or may not have included a change in marital status, from one survey year to the next. Preliminary analyses revealed that CFS was a more robust measure than change in marital status. In most survey years CFS accounted for greater variance in the income-to-poverty ratio (IPR) than that accounted for by change in marital status. Hence, I retained CFS as a correlate in the regression models for IPR and further examined and reported results regarding changes in marital status when warranted. In general, a reduction in family size was expected to be correlated with greater economic well-being (Blank, 1997). Given that many married women lose economic standing upon separation or divorce, however, it was expected that for some of them, a reduction in family size would result in less economic well-being (Burggraf, 1997; Rodgers, 1990; Weitzman, 1988).

The other change variable, change in the number of hours worked from one survey year to the next (CHWK), was used to assess the extent to which effects of changes in work effort on economic well-being might be augmented or offset by the number of hours worked (HOWK) in a given year. In general, changes in work effort were expected to be positively related to economic well-being: an increase or decrease in CHWK would be correlated with a corresponding change in the income-to-poverty ratio (IPR). However, CHWK might be inversely related to IPR if, for example, a respondent received a higher rate of pay or if other family income increased sufficiently from one year to the next such that a decrease in hours worked did not adversely affect economic well-being. Fortunately, rate of pay was a variable in the NLSY data files, thereby permitting further analysis of findings when necessary.

The psychological variables comprised scores of two commonly used measures for individual initiative and self-esteem. The Rotter locus-of-control scale (LOC) captured individual initiative. This scale was designed to measure the extent to which one perceived a causal relationship between his or her own behavior and subsequent events. At one extreme were those who believe that environmental factors like luck, chance, or fate control their lives (external control). At the other extreme were those who believe they have control over their lives through self-motivation or self-determination (internal control). Empirical evidence for the relationship of achievement and autonomy to the Rotter scale came from research conducted by Rotter (1966 and 1975) and others (Boor, 1974; Watson, 1981). Scores ranged between 8 and 16. Higher scores signified belief in more external control, and hence weak belief in self-determination or a lack of individual initiative. Given the emphasis on individual effort and portended rewards associated with the range of supply-side incentives espoused throughout the period as part of the Reagan revolution (Anderson, 1988), the relation between LOC and the income-to-poverty ratio (IPR) was expected to be inverse. That is, those who scored on the lower end of the Rotter internal-external locus of control scale, thereby demonstrating more internal control, self-determination, or individual initiative, were expected to have higher levels of economic well-being than those with higher scores indicative of more external control or a greater belief in fate.

The second of the two psychological variables, the Rosenberg self-esteem scale (SELF EST), captured the degree of approval or disapproval toward oneself (Rosenberg, 1965). Wilson, Ellwood, and Brooks-Gunn (1995) have noted that the role of self-esteem in economic well-being remains somewhat ambiguous. There is no consensus regarding measurement and, to the extent positive events improve self-esteem and negative ones diminish it, cause and effect are difficult to distinguish. The scale used here, however, has demonstrated high internal consistency with reliability coefficients ranging from .84 (Strocchia-Rivera, 1988) to .87 (Menaghan, 1990), depending on the nature of the NLSY sample selected. It contained ten statements of self approval or disapproval with which respondents were asked to strongly agree, agree, disagree, or strongly disagree. Scores ranged from 1 "Strongly Agree" to 4 "Strongly Disagree." With appropriate reverse scoring of five items, such as "I wish I had more self-respect" and "I feel useless at times," higher scores signified greater self-esteem. The 1980 scores were used for study year 1980; the 1987 scores, for study years 1987 and 1993. It should be noted, however, that the correlation between the 1980 and 1987 self-esteem scores, based on the entire cohort who reported on all scale items in both years (n = 9,918), was moderately positive (r = .47), signifying that this measure may be less reliable as time passes between measurements. Hence, although findings are reported for 1993, subsequent discussion of the correlation between self-esteem and economic well-being was confined primarily to 1987. Given findings from previous research emphasizing the overwhelming influence of demographic factors and labor market conditions on economic well-being, self-esteem was thought to have at best a weakly positive or no correlation with the income-to-poverty ratio (IPR) in 1980, while it was expected to exhibit a moderately positive relationship with IPR in 1987 and 1993.

Procedures

First, I show the income-to-poverty ratios (IPRs) by year for the entire study sample and then stratified by sex and ethnicity/race. Second, the results of time series analysis using simple regression indicate the secular trend in the IPR by sex and ethnicity/race between 1979 and 1993. As in Chapter 1, I report the Coefficient of Determination (r^2) and the Durbin-Watson Statistic (*d*) for autocorrelation. Again, if *d* is close to 2, it is assumed that autocorrelation is not a problem. To the extent autocorrelation is problematic, the slope and strength of the coefficients are less reliable, as is the predictive ability of the regression model. Third, to determine if economic well-being as measured by the IPR differed among sex and ethnicity/race groups by class, the general linear model (GLM) procedure was conducted separately on affluent and poor families for each of the 15 study years. As noted in Chapter 1, the GLM is used with unbalanced designs, that is, when cell sizes are unequal, as is the case among the sex and ethnicity/race groups. When appropriate for post hoc analysis of economic well-being between pairs of the six sex and ethnicity/race groups, the LSMEANS procedure was used. The F ratio, follow-up pairwise comparisons, and results of their respective tests of statistical significance are reported.

Fourth and finally, to assess the influence of demographic, human capital, and psychological characteristics on economic well-being, I used multiple regression analysis. The income-to-poverty ratio (IPR) was the criterion variable. Table 2.1 describes the background (AGE R, HGC R, HGC RM, HOWK, MS, R SMSA, and UNEMP R), change (CFS and CHWK), and psychological (LOC and SELF EST) variables constituting the correlates used in the regression models reported for selected years 1980, 1987, and 1993. To indicate how much the IPR would change for every 1-unit change in each of the respective correlate-variables, I reported the nonstandardized multiple regression coefficient (*b*). I also reported the uniqueness indices (UI) and accompanying F value that tested the statistical significance of each uniqueness index. The UI signified the percentage of variance in the IPR accounted for by a given correlate beyond the variance accounted for by the other ten in the model (Hatcher and Stepanski, 1994).

In the main body of the text, I reported results only for those variables found to be statistically significant for the entire study sample and when the study sample was stratified by sex and ethnicity/race for the selected years 1980, 1987, and 1993. Results of full regression models for the entire study sample, as well as stratified by sex and ethnicity/race, for 1980, 1987, and 1993 can be found in the Appendix, Tables A.1 - A.21. In addition to the *b*s and UIs, the full models also report the standardized multiple regression coefficients (Beta or B weight) and the accompanying *t* tests that tested the statistical significance of each coefficient, thereby showing the relative or rank-order contribution of each correlate to the IPR. It should be emphasized that the regression results are meant to be construed as correlative not causal in nature. That is, they indicate the amount of variation in the measure of economic well-being that can be attributed to the correlates which in this regard might be better construed as predictors rather than as causal factors (Hatcher and Stepanski, 1994; Lieberson, 1985; Stevens, 1986). Hence, cause-and-effect inferences per se would be inappropriate given the statistical procedures used here.

Results

Levels and Trends in Economic Well-Being. Table 2.2 shows the mean income-to-poverty ratios (IPRs), while Table 2.3 shows the respective Percent Changes, Coefficients of Determination and the Durbin-Watson Statistic for the IPR between 1979 and 1993, by sex and ethnicity/race.

Table 2.2 *Income-to-Poverty Ratio, 1979-1993, by Sex and Ethnicity/Race*

		Male			Female		
Year	Total	Black	White	Hispanic	Black	White	Hispanic
1979	2.79	1.93	3.62	2.50	1.81	3.30	2.28
1980	2.79	1.98	3.60	2.96	1.77	3.21	2.27
1981	2.81	2.07	3.68	2.77	1.84	3.18	2.35
1982	2.59	1.98	3.31	2.65	1.63	2.99	2.16
1983	2.64	2.03	3.42	2.81	1.64	3.03	2.15
1984	2.86	2.15	3.72	2.82	1.85	3.26	2.42
1985	3.01	2.47	3.76	3.26	1.95	3.37	2.58
1986	3.14	2.50	3.92	3.24	2.01	3.64	2.58
1987	3.32	2.60	4.19	3.41	2.07	3.85	2.68
1988	3.40	2.73	4.24	3.42	2.32	3.86	2.74
1989	3.47	2.99	4.40	3.60	2.30	3.79	2.89
1990	3.37	2.69	4.36	3.60	2.15	3.74	2.89
1991	3.34	2.84	4.24	3.28	2.13	3.70	3.03
1992	3.29	2.72	4.24	3.37	2.09	3.63	2.84
1993	3.43	3.01	4.22	3.65	2.27	3.80	2.99

Table 2.3 *Percent Change, Coefficients, and Durbin-Watson Statistic for the Income-to-Poverty Ratio, 1979-1993, by Sex and Ethnicity/Race*

	Male				Female		
Statistics	Total	Black	White	Hispanic	Black	White	Hispanic
% Change	30	60	17	46	25	15	31
b	0.061	0.612	0.111	0.088	0.046	0.045	0.063
T	6.708[a]	9.85[a]	4.708[a]	5.756[a]	2.04	1.98[a]	9.02[a]
r^2	0.78	.88	0.63	0.72	0.24	0.23	0.86
d	0.61	1.44	1.39	1.63	1.71	2.56	1.27

Note: Percent change reflects the difference between the income-to-poverty ratio in 1979 and 1993. For the Durbin-Watson Statistic, with the number of independent variables k = 1 and n = 15, the critical values for comparing *d* at the .05 level of statistical significance are such that there is evidence of positive autocorrelation when $d < .81$ and of negative autocorrelation when $d > 3.19$.

[a] $p < .001$

As Tables 2.2 and 2.3 show, the income-to-poverty ratio (IPR) for the entire youth cohort increased by 30% from 2.79 to 3.43. Although time accounted for 78% of the variance in IPR, the aggregate positive secular trend was found to be autocorrelated ($r^2 = .78$, $d = 0.61$, $b = .061$). Hence, the finding of an upward trend in economic well-being cannot be considered reliable. Disaggregating the data by sex and ethnicity/race, however, produced significant positive trends for everyone except black women. Black males had the greatest increase in IPR, 60%, between 1979 and 1993, followed by Hispanic males. White males had the second smallest increase in IPR, 17%, signifying an overall modest trend between 1979 and 1993.

Hispanic females had the fourth greatest increase in IPR, 31%, between

1979 and 1993, reflecting, like black and Hispanic males, a strong positive trend. White women had the smallest percentage increase in IPR, 15%, signifying a weak positive trend.

The degree of change and the intensity of trend in the income-to-poverty ratio (IPR) reflected in part the level of economic well-being in 1979 by sex and ethnicity/race. White males, for example, had the greatest level of economic well-being in 1979, with family incomes more than three and one-half times the poverty level (IPR = 3.62), while black women had the lowest (IPR = 1.81). As noted, the upward trend was strongest for black men. As Table 2.4 shows, white males enjoyed the greatest level of economic well-being of all ethnicity/race groups in each year between 1979 and 1993, except 1986 and 1987.

Table 2.4 *Rank Order of Mean Income-to-Poverty Ratio Differences, 1979-1993, by Sex and Ethnicity/Race (n = 2745)*

Year	Sex and Ethnicity/Race	F
1979	WM >WF[a] >HM[a], HF, BM[c], BF; HM >BM[b]; HM >BF[a]	73.92[a]
1980	WM > WF[a], HM > HF[a], BM, BF; HF > BF[b]	71.73[a]
1981	WM > WF[a]> HM[b]> HF[a], BM, BF; HF > BF[b]	66.56[a]
1982	WM > WF[a]> HMc> HF[b], BM> BF[b]	66.48[a]
1983	WM > WF[a] , HM > HF[c] , BM > BF[b]	67.98[a]
1984	WM > WF[a]> HM[b]> HF, BM> BF[c]	67.03[a]
1985	WM > WF[a], HM > HF[b], BM > BF[a]	54.10[a]
1986	WM, WF[c]> HM > HF[b], BM > BF[b]	58.64[a]
1987	WM, WF[b]>HM > HF[b], BM > BF[b]	64.89[a]
1988	WM > WF[b]>HM[c] > HF[c], BM> BF[c]	56.23[a]
1989	WM > Wf[a], HM > BM[b] , HF > BF[b]	54.69[a]
1990	WM > WF[a], HM > HF[b], BM > BF[a]	67.12[a]
1991	WM > Wf[a]> HM, HF, BM > BF[a] ; HM > BM[c]	63.03[a]
1992	WM > WF[a], HM > HF[c], BM > BF[c]	72.28[a]
1993	WM > WF[a], HM > BM[a], HF > BF[a]	62.94[a]

Legend: BM = Black Male, WM = White Male, HM = Hispanic Male, BF = Black Female, WF = White Female, HF = Hispanic Female

[a] $p < .001$; [b] $p<.01$; [c] $p < .05$

White males lived in families with incomes more than three and one-half times the poverty threshold in 1979 (IPR = 3.63) and nearly four and one-quarter times in 1993 (IPR = 4.22). Despite a modest trend increase, the economic well-being of white males, as measured by the income-to-poverty ratio (IPR), exceeded that of any other group to a statistically significant degree in all but two years between 1979 and 1993.

White females enjoyed sole possession of the second greatest levels of economic well-being in eight of the fifteen study years. They shared the second highest level in economic well-being in the other seven study years with Hispanic males. With the exception of 1982, white females lived in families whose income exceeded three times the poverty threshold, as did Hispanic males after 1984. Black women, on the other hand, consistently lived in families at the lowest level of economic well-being. They reached the lowest level of all groups at any time in 1982 when their family income was slightly more than one and one-half the poverty line (IPR = 1.63) and their highest level in 1993 when it was slightly more than two and one-quarter times the poverty threshold (IPR = 2.27).

Correlates of Economic Well-Being for Selected Years. Table 2.5 shows the regression coefficient (*b*) and Uniqueness Index (UI) for selected years 1980, 1987, and 1993. As noted, *b* signifies by how much economic well-being, as measured by the income-to-poverty ratio (IPR), will change for every 1-unit change in the correlate-variable, while the UI represents the percentage of variance in IPR accounted for by a given correlate beyond that of the other ten correlates. (The full regression models and accompanying tests of statistical significance upon which results in Table 2.5 are based can be found in the Appendix, Tables A.1-A.21.) The year 1980 was selected because it was the first year that incorporated change variables from the earliest preceding year containing sufficiently complete information about the respondents and because it represented the period when most of the cohort was still considered youth, that is, under 25 years of age. The year 1987 was selected because self-esteem was measured a second time. In 1987, the median age was 27 years old. The year 1993 was selected because nearly an equal number of years separated it from 1980, the first measure of self-esteem, and from 1987, the second measure of self-esteem. In addition, 1993 was the most recent year of available data. Although the most recent survey year was 1994, many relevant questions, like family income, referred to the previous calendar year. In 1993, the median age of the study sample was 33 and, with the youngest at age 30, all respondents were considered in their mature or prime working years (usually considered between 25 and 54 years of age).

For each selected year, the seven background, two change, and two psychological variables were regressed on the income-to-poverty ratio (IPR). For the entire study sample, the full regression models accounted for 16% of the variance in IPR in 1980 ($F = 48.12$, $p < .001$), 28% in 1987 ($F = 97.35$, $p < .001$), and 29% in 1993 ($F = 99.66$, $p < .001$), while variance in IPR accounted for by the full models stratified by sex and ethnicity/race ranged from a low of 6% for white males in 1980 ($F = 3.92$, $p = .001$) to a high of 44% for Hispanic females in 1987 ($F = 15.44$, $p = .001$), with a median of 27% and an average of 26%. As noted, Table 2.5 shows only the regression coefficient (*b*) and Uniqueness Index (UI) for each statistically significant correlate for selected years 1980, 1987, and 1993, by sex and ethnicity/race; other related information about the full models can be found in the Appendix, Tables A.1-A.21. This analysis proceeds by reviewing the findings based on the total study sample, then by showing differences by sex and ethnicity/race.

Table 2.5 *Nonstandardized Regression Coefficient and Percentage () of Variance in Economic Well-Being Accounted for by a Given Correlate Beyond That of Others, Selected Years, by Sex and Ethnicity/Race*

		1980					
		Male			Female		
Descriptors:	Total	Black	White	Hispanic	Black	White	Hispanic
Age R				.198 (1.8)			
HGC R	.114 (0.5)					.205 (1.2)	
HGC RM	.130 (3.2)	.124 (4.6)	.121 (1.2)	.967 (3.5)	.097 (2.1)	.058 (2.5)	.078 (2.7)
HOWK (10^{-2})	.608 (4.7)	.398 (3.3)	.457 (2.0)		.552 (4.9)	.506 (2.3)	.437 (2.9)
MS (1=married)							
R SMSA (1=within SMSA)			.206 (0.7)				
UNEMP R	-.010 (0.1)			-.370 (2.0)			
Change Variables:							
CFS	-.126 (1.1)	-.147 (3.5)		-.391 (10.6)	-.102 (1.5)	-.112 (0.7)	-.193 (4.8)
CHWK (10^{-2})	-.339 (0.9)				-.325 (1.1)	-.411 (1.1)	
Psychological Variables:							
LOC							
SELF EST	.033 (0.4)	.038 (1.0)			.034 (0.7)		.076 (2.6)

Note: The full regression models and accompanying tests of statistical significance upon which these data are based can be found in Appendix A, Tables A.1 - A.21. Only the Regression Coefficient and Uniqueness Index of those correlates that met statistical significance are shown here.

Table 2.5 *Regression Coefficient and Percentage () of Variance in Economic Well-being Accounted for by a Given Correlate Beyond That of Others, Selected Years, by Sex and Ethnicity/Race continued*

1987

			Male			Female	
Correlates::	Total	Black	White	Hispanic	Black	White	Hispanic
Background Variables:							
AGE R							
HGC R	.241 (3.5)	.163 (2.4)	.246 (3.4)	.204 (3.4)	.155 (2.3)	.313 (4.3)	.169 (3.8)
HGC RM	.083 (0.9)	.072 (0.9)				.100 (0.6)	
HOWK (10^{-2})	.773 (6.9)	.686 (8.1)	.865 (4.4)	.600 (3.5)	.613 (8.6)	.859 (6.3)	.835 (9.5)
MS (1=married)	.646 (1.5)				.647 (3.1)	.762 (1.5)	.780 (3.1)
R SMSA (1= within SMSA)	.519 (0.6)		.704 (1.0)			.896 (1.5)	
UNEMP R	-.144 (0.2)			-.581 (5.1)	-.190 (0.7)		-.338 (2.2)
Change Variables:							
CFS	-.203 (0.9)	-.135 (1.3)	-.518 (3.3)		-.106 (0.8)	-.212 (0.4)	
CHWK (10^{-2})	-.359 (0.6)		-.515 (1.0)		-.222 (0.6)	-.439 (0.7)	
Psychological Variables:							
LOC	-.065 (0.1)				-.101 (0.9)		
SELF EST	.048 (0.5)		.055 (0.6)			.076 (1.1)	.074 (1.6)

Note: The full regression models and accompanying tests of statistical significance upon which these data are based can be found in Appendix A, Tables A.1 - A.21. Only the Regression Coefficient and Uniqueness Index of those correlates that met statistical significance are shown here.

Table 2.5 *Regression Coefficient and Percentage () of Variance in Economic Well-being Accounted for by a Given Correlate Beyond That of Others, Selected Years, by Sex and Ethnicity/Race continued*

1993

		Male			Female		
Correlates::	Total	Black	White	Hispanic	Black	White	Hispanic
Background Variables:							
AGE R							
HGC R	.256 (6.7)	.291 (6.2)	.247 (5.3)	.219 (5.1)	.225 (5.7)	.317 (8.6)	.168 (5.4)
HGC RM	.057 (0.6)						
HOWK (10^{-2})	.682 (6.8)	.569 (5.7)	.580 (2.7)		.549 (8.2)	.669 (7.2)	.612 (7.8)
MS (1=married)	.389 (0.7)		-.517 (1.0)		.467 (1.6)		.481 (1.5)
R SMSA							
(1=within SMSA)	.619 (1.2)		1.081 (3.6)			.783 (2.0)	
UNEMP R							
Change Variables:							
CFS	-.104 (0.1)				-.146 (0.6)		
CHWK (10^{-2})	-.171 (0.2)					-.304 (0.5)	
Psychological Variables:							
LOC	-.050 (0.1)				-.083 (0.6)		
SELF EST	.028 (0.2)	.068 (1.6)					

Note: The full regression models and accompanying tests of statistical significance upon which these data are based can be found in Appendix A, Tables A.1 - A.21. Only the Regression Coefficient and Uniqueness Index of those correlates that met statistical significance are shown here.

Variation in Correlates of Economic Well-Being. As Table 2.5 shows, for the entire study sample, hours worked (HOWK) accounted for the greatest variance beyond that of the other ten correlates in 1980 (4.7%), 1987 (6.9%), and 1993 (6.8%). In each of these years the direction was positive, signifying, as expected, that increased work effort in a given year correlated with improved economic well-being. Each 600 additional hours worked in 1980 produced a 1-unit increase in the income-to-poverty ratio (IPR), that is, an additional 100% increase in family income above the poverty threshold. Comparable figures were 770 hours for 1987 and 690 hours for 1993. Also as expected, highest grade completed of respondents (HGC R) accounted for the second greatest variance in IPR in 1987 (3.5%) and 1993 (6.7%), when most of the cohort had finished their formal education, whereas in 1980 when the cohort was still youthful, family background factors indexed by the highest grade completed of respondents' mothers (HGC RM) accounted for the second greatest variance in IPR, 3.2%.

For the entire sample, the remaining variables accounted for roughly equitable, but relatively negligible, amounts of variance in the income-to-poverty ratio (IPR) in each of the selected years. Marital status (MS), for example, accounted for the third greatest amount of variance in IPR in 1987 (1.5%) and in 1993 (0.7%). MS was positively correlated with IPR, signifying that married youth had greater levels of economic well-being in their more mature years than those who were not married

In all three years, both change in family size (CFS) and change in hours worked (CHWK) also accounted for roughly equivalent variance in the income-to-poverty ratio (IPR) and both were inversely related to economic well-being. In 1980, for example, with each reduction of work effort on the part of respondents by about 125 hours from that of 1979, families experienced a 1-unit increase in the IPR, that is, an additional 100% increase in family income above the poverty threshold. Comparable figures were 359 in 1987 and 171 in 1993.

These findings appeared somewhat paradoxical in light of the positive relation between the income-to-poverty ratio (IPR) and the number of hours worked in a given year (HOWK). The measure of economic well-being used in this study, however, accounts for family size, and the inverse relation between IPR and change in hours worked (CHWK) was nonetheless consistent with the negative relationship found between IPR and change in family size (CFS). Decreased family size from one year to the next was found to be related to greater economic well-being. To the extent exits from the family had little or no adverse impact on total family income, then one's economic well-being as measured by IPR could actually rise while work effort decreased. Close to the same amount of family income could support fewer people at a higher level of economic well-being. In separate analyses (not shown), change in marital status was substituted for CFS in the regression model for each study year and was found to account for no variance in IPR beyond that of the other ten correlates in any year.

Finally, though negligible, both psychological variables accounted for variance in the income-to-poverty ratio (IPR). Internal-external locus of control (LOC) accounted for variance in IPR beyond that of the other ten correlates in 1987 (0.1%) and 1993 (0.1%). The direction was negative in both years, signifying that as the cohort matured, those who demonstrated greater internal control, that is, who believed they have control over their lives through self-motivation or self-determination, enjoyed greater levels of economic well-being than those with more external control. Self-esteem accounted for variance in IPR beyond that of the other ten correlates in 1980 (0.4%), 1987 (0.5%), and 1993 (0.2%). In each year, the direction was positive, signifying that greater self-esteem was correlated with greater levels of economic well-being.

Variation in Correlates of Economic Well-Being by Sex and Ethnicity/Race.

Background Variables. As can be seen in Table 2.5, correlates of the income-to-poverty ratio (IPR) varied by sex and ethnicity/race. In 1980, among family background measures, only highest grade completed of respondents' mothers (HGC RM) accounted for variance in IPR beyond that of the other ten correlates for all groups, varying by sex and ethnicity/race. The direction was always positive, signifying that greater levels of mothers' education, and by extension greater family background resources in general, were associated with greater economic well-being while the cohort was still considered youthful.

As expected, the highest grade completed of the respondent (HGC R) was positively related to economic well-being for the entire cohort in 1980, 1987, and 1993. In 1980, however, HGC R accounted for variance in the income-to-poverty ratio (IPR) beyond that of the other ten correlates only for white females (1.2%). Given the significance of mothers' level of education (HGC RM) and the youthfulness of cohort in 1980, that the respondents' education level was correlated with the economic well-being of any sub-group came as a surprise. A partial explanation lay in the relationship between levels of education and economic well-being. As noted, white males lived in families with the highest levels of economic well-being to a statistically significant degree more than any other sex and ethnicity/race group. A separate GLM (not shown), however, revealed that in 1980 white males and females had completed equivalent grades of education, 12.12 and 12.10 years respectively, and both of these were greater than levels achieved by any other sex and ethnicity/race group to a statistically significant degree. Because white men lived in families with such high levels of economic well-being, their educational level accounted for little variance when controlling for other factors. Given the same level of education as white males, that of white females was correlated with lesser levels of economic well-being when controlling for the same factors. In 1987 and 1993, HGC R accounted for variance in IPR beyond that of the other ten correlates for all groups. In 1993, HGC R accounted for the highest percentages of variance in the IPR for all groups except black and Hispanic females, for whom number of hours worked (HOWK) was more important.

In 1980, the number of hours worked (HOWK) accounted for the greatest variance in the income to poverty ratio (IPR) for white males (2.0%) and black females (4.9%), the second greatest for Hispanic females (2.9%) and white females (2.3%), and the third greatest for black males (3.3%). In 1987, HOWK accounted for the greatest variance in IPR beyond that of the other ten correlates for all groups. HOWK again accounted for variance in IPR beyond that of the other ten correlates in 1993 for all groups except Hispanic males.

Although marital status (MS) accounted for variance in the income-to-poverty ratio (IPR) in 1987 and 1993 for the total study sample and had a positive direction in both years, it varied considerably when controlling for sex and ethnicity/race. MS accounted for no variation in IPR for males in 1987 and only for white males in 1993. In 1987 and 1993, MS accounted for more variation in IPR among black (3.1% and 8.2% respectively) and Hispanic (3.1% and 7.8%) than white (1.5% and 7.2%) women. The direction for each group was positive, signifying that married women in 1987 and 1993 enjoyed greater economic well-being than those not married. The direction between IPR and MS for white males in 1993, however, was negative, signifying that married men had lower levels of economic well-being than unmarried men. As Table 2.6 indicates, this finding was in part a function of greater family income and relatively similar or smaller family size of white males in 1993 compared to all other groups.

Table 2.6 *Family Size, Income, and Percent Difference, 1987 and 1993, by Marital Status, Sex and Ethnicity/Race*

	White Males				Other			
	Married		Not Married		Married		Not Married	
Year	Family Size	Family Income	Family Size	Family Income	Family Size	Family Income	Family Size	Family Income
1987	3.15	$41,699	2.05	$34,108	3.59	$37,689	3.07	$24,484
1993	3.65	$77,296	1.88	$52,536	3.99	$68,840	2.88	$41,021
% Difference	15.87	85.37	-8.29	54.03	11.14	82.65	-6.19	67.54

As noted, marital status (MS) accounted for no variation in the income-to-poverty ratio (IPR) beyond that of the other correlates in 1987. As Table 2.6 shows, in 1987, the family income of unmarried white males was roughly comparable to that of married others, while family size was the smallest of all groups. In 1993, the family income of unmarried white males was somewhat less comparable than that of other married males and females, while family size had nonetheless decreased the most, by over 8%, albeit from the smallest base. Divorce, as an accompanying factor in the decline of family size, varied somewhat by sex and ethnicity/race. The divorce rate among those who lived in smaller families in 1993 than in 1992 was 8% for black males, 29% for white males, 29% for Hispanic males, 19% for black females, 22% for white females, and 28% for Hispanic females. Concomitantly, substantial majorities of those who divorced between 1992 and 1993 lived in smaller families in 1993: 76% of black males, 78% of white males, 75% of Hispanic males, 64% of black females, 82% of white females, and 77% of Hispanic females.

Although divorce resulted in reduced family size for roughly comparable majorities of each sex and ethnicity/race group, the more varied but substantially lower rates of divorce among those who lived in smaller families signified that other types of exits from families accounted for smaller family size, even for white males. Nonetheless, white males and Hispanic males had the highest rates of divorce among those who lived in smaller families, suggesting that the improved economic well-being that accompanied the reduction of family size for white men in 1993 reflected the greater proportion of their individual or wage-related contribution to total family income than that for other groups. A separate analysis using the GLM procedure (not shown), indicated that this was the case for all but Hispanic males. In 1993, 71% of total family income for white men came from their wages, compared to 66% for Hispanic males from whom there was no statistically significant difference, 55% for black males, 47% for black females, 37% for Hispanic females, and 36% for white females. Because Hispanic males lived in larger families than white males, their economic well-being did not necessarily improve with a decrease in family size between 1992 and 1993, even though their wage-related income was not different to a statistically significant degree from that of white males. Hence, white men benefited economically from reduced family size between 1992 and 1993, while others did not, because of the combination of two factors: their wage contribution to total family income was so high and their family size so small.

Residence (R SMSA) accounted for variance in the income-to-poverty ratio (IPR) beyond that of the other ten correlates in 1980 only for white males (0.7%) and in 1987 and 1993 only for white males (1.0% and 3.6% respectively) and white females (1.5% and 2.0% respectively). The direction was always positive, signifying that among these families those who resided within Standard Metropolitan Statistical Areas had higher levels of economic well-being than those who resided outside SMSAs. In part, these differences, among white males and females, in economic well-being between those who resided within SMSAs from those outside SMSAs reflected greater rates of pay. Separate *t* tests of hourly rates of pay by R SMSA (not shown) revealed that white males who lived in families within SMSAs had much higher (unadjusted) hourly rates of pay in 1993 ($16.60) and 1987 ($10.98) than those who lived in families outside SMSAs ($11.09 and $8.00 respectively) and that women did likewise, in 1993 ($13.67 compared to $8.19) and in 1987 ($7.40 compared to $5.80). Finally, the unemployment rate in the area of residence (UNEMP R) accounted for variance in IPR beyond that of the other ten correlates in 1980 only for Hispanic males (2.0%) and in 1987 for Hispanic males (5.1%), black females (0.7%), and Hispanic females (2.2%). In 1980 and 1987, the direction was negative, signifying that lower rates of unemployment were correlated with greater economic well-being. In 1987, the average rates of unemployment in their respective areas of residence were virtually indistinguishable by sex and ethnicity/race, ranging from a high of 3.2% for Hispanic females to a low of 2.8% for black males and females. No relationship was found between UNEMP R and IPR in 1993 for any sub-group.

Change Variables. Changes in family size (CFS) and hours worked (CHWK) from the preceding year accounted for variation in the income-to-poverty ratio (IPR). CFS accounted for variation in IPR beyond that of the other ten correlates for black males in 1980 and 1987, white males in 1987, Hispanic males in 1980, black females in all three years, white females in 1980 and 1987, and Hispanic females only in 1980. In all instances, the direction of the relationship between CFS and IPR was negative, signifying that decreases in family sizes were correlated with increases in economic well-being. The magnitude of any given decrease was in part a function of family size. In general, the smaller the base from which family size may have changed from one survey year to the next, the greater the regression coefficient.

Change in hours worked (CHWK) also accounted for variance in the income-to-poverty ratio (IPR) in 1980 only for black and white females, in 1987 for white males and black and white females, and in 1993 only for white females. In each instance, the direction of change was inversely related to IPR, signifying that members of these groups who worked less from one survey year to the next nonetheless enjoyed greater economic well-being. As noted previously in regard to the total study sample, the inverse relation between IPR and

CHWK was consistent with the negative relationship found between IPR and change in family size (CFS). With the exception of white females in 1993, all groups having an inverse relationship between CHWK and IPR also decreased their family size from the preceding year. To the extent that exits from these families had little or no adverse impact on total family income, then one's economic well-being as measured by IPR rose while work effort decreased. In 1993, white women lived in families whose size remained relatively stable, increasing to an average of 3.47 from 3.43 members in 1992.

Presumably income from other sources such as husbands or partners, or a higher rate of pay, enabled white women in 1993 to work less than they did in 1992 yet enjoy even greater economic well-being. Separate *t* test procedures ruled out the likely influences of income from husbands or partners and suggested that higher rates of pay enabled white women to work less and enjoy greater economic well-being. For those white women who had spouses or partners for both years, the percentage increases of the spouses' or partners' wages of those whose hours of work declined in 1993 from 1992 were both substantively negligible and statistically insignificant from those whose hours of work remained the same or increased (7.78% and 9.17% respectively). White women whose hours of work decreased between 1993 and 1992 had a substantive, though not statistically significant increase of 67% in their rate of pay compared to a 7% increase for those who worked the same number of hours. Finally, white women whose hours of work decreased were as likely to be newly married (and hence the potential beneficiaries of a second source of income) as women whose hours of work remained the same.

Psychological Variables. Psychological variables also accounted for variance in the income-to-poverty ratio (IPR) beyond that of other correlates, although, when they did, it was usually in the smallest amounts. Internal-external locus of control (LOC) accounted for no variance in IPR beyond that of the other ten correlates in 1980 and only for black females both in 1987 and 1993. The direction of the relationship between LOC and IPR was negative, signifying that as the black women matured, those who demonstrated greater internal control, that is, a stronger belief in self-determination or individual initiative, enjoyed greater levels of economic well-being than those with more external control.

This finding for black women failed to confirm much previous research showing little or no relationship of psychological attributes in general and internal-external locus of control (LOC) in particular with economic well-being (Caputo, 1998; Dolinsky, Caputo, and O'Kane, 1989; Duncan 1984; Danziger and Gottschalk, 1993 and 1995; Gottschalk, McLanahan, and Sandefur, 1994). Given that the work effort of black women was not related to the economic well-being of their families in 1993, this finding suggested that the role of beliefs about control of one's life through self-determination extended beyond that usually attributed to increased wages. A separate *t* test procedure between those black women whose hourly rate of pay increased and those for whom it either remained the same or decreased between 1992 and 1993 showed no statistically significant difference on LOC. Likewise, separate *t* test procedures between those black women whose work effort declined and those whose work effort remained constant or increased between 1992 and 1993 showed no differences in the measure of internal-external locus of control, being newly married, their hourly rates of pay in 1993, the percentage change in their hourly rates of pay, nor the percentage change in their spouses' or partners' wages.

Paradoxically, these findings about young black women suggested that beliefs about control over one's life through self-determination might play its most important role among those who lived in families with the lowest levels of economic well-being and with the least related gains throughout the study period and that beyond a certain level or threshold of economic well-being such beliefs cease to matter. To determine whether class mattered more than sex and ethnicity/race in this regard, seven dichotomized variables were created to distinguish those who lived above a specified level of economic well-being from those who lived at or below that level. One such dichotomized variable, for example, was coded such that those whose income-to-poverty ratio (IPR) was greater than seven times the poverty threshold, = 1, while all others = 0; a second, such that those whose IPR > six times the poverty threshold, = 1, while all others = 0; a third, such that those whose IPR > five times the poverty threshold, = 1, while all others = 0; and so on.

Separate *t* tests of each of these seven variables were then used to determine if differences in the measure for internal-external locus of control could be found when controlling for sex and ethnicity/race. To the extent such differences could be found among all groups, the more likely beliefs about the control of one's life through self-determination reflect differences by class rather than by sex and ethnicity/race. However, to the extent such differences could be found among black women but not among others, such beliefs might matter beyond an identifiable threshold of economic well-being only for black women. To the extent such differences cannot be found, such beliefs could be considered crucial for young, maturing black women, the most economically disadvantaged group in the sample, regardless of class.

Results of the *t* tests (not shown) revealed statistically significant differences in the measure of internal-external locus of control in the expected direction on each of the six dichotomized variables only for black women. That is, regardless of the value of the income-to-poverty ratio (IPR), 1 through 7, when compared against all others of lower economic well-being, those black women who lived in more affluent families had a stronger belief about control of their lives through self-determination than did those who lived in less affluent families. This was not the case for any other group, except Hispanic women, for whom, like black women in 1993, work effort was not inversely related to economic well-being, but for whom, unlike black women, the measure of internal-external locus of control did not account for variance in economic well-being beyond that of other factors. In addition, Hispanic women lived in families with higher levels of economic well-being than black women. These findings support the case that beliefs about control of one's life through self-determination play a significant role in the economic well-being of young, maturing black women, the most economically disadvantaged group in the sample, regardless of class.

Self-esteem (SELF EST) also accounted for variance in the income-to-poverty ratio (IPR) beyond that of the other ten correlates in 1980 for black males, black females, and Hispanic females; in 1987, for white males, white females, and Hispanic females; and in 1993 only for black males. In all instances, the direction of the relationship between IPR and SELF EST was positive, signifying that greater self-esteem was correlated with greater levels of economic well-being. Neither internal-external locus of control (LOC) nor SELF EST accounted for variance in IPR for Hispanic males in 1980, 1987, or 1993. Given that most of the cohort lived in their parents' households in 1980 and that the 1993 results might be too dubious since six years had elapsed from the second measurement of self-esteem in 1987, subsequent discussion of self-esteem is limited to the significant results found for white males and females and Hispanic females in 1987 when most of the cohort were in their early prime working years.

Discussion

Results of Chapter 1 suggested that the economic circumstances of affluent and poor families among the youth cohort improved, albeit at different rates when accounting for sex and ethnicity/race, between 1979 and 1993. Despite these gains at the extreme ends of the economic continuum, results of Chapter 2, which examined the entire cohort, revealed somewhat of a less rosy scenario. No overall improvement in the economic well-being of the cohort was found to a statistically significant degree, although the general direction was positive or upward. As the economy expanded throughout the period, for this cohort of youth economic well-being improved for those at the top and bottom rungs of the economic ladder. Unlike the upper rung of the economic ladder, the lower tier of the cohort went against the grain of the general population, for whom poverty failed to decline and average incomes fell (Caputo, 1995b; U.S. Bureau of the Census, 1997). Results of this chapter also suggested that the well-being of those in the middle was neither necessarily better nor worse. In this regard, the cohort resembled the general working population, namely middle-income families and workers were economically stagnant throughout much of the 1980s and early 1990s (Blank, 1997; Levy, 1995; Levy and Michel, 1991; Madrick, 1995). As with many aggregate portraits, however, this one masked significant, albeit differential, gains within the cohort when accounting for sex and ethnicity/race. Economic well-being improved to varying degrees for all sex and ethnicity/race sub-groups of the cohort except black women.

The inability of young black women to position themselves in more favorable economic circumstances as they matured is a glaring result that raises issues regarding the disproportionate numbers of single-headed families, particularly among those in poverty (Blank, 1997; Hernandez, 1997; McLanahan and Garfinkel, 1997; Rodgers,

1990). Black women started out in families with the lowest levels of economic well-being and essentially remained there. Although black men also started out in families with lower levels of economic well-being than all other groups, except black women, as they matured they nonetheless positioned themselves in families whose economic circumstances improved to a statistically significant degree. The combination of sex and ethnicity/race appeared to be detrimental to the economic fortunes of young black women. All things considered, as the cohort of youth matured throughout the 1980s and 1990s, black males were able to take advantage of the expanding economy, while black women at best lost no ground. Given that the economic circumstances of others improved to some degree as the economy expanded, remaining in place economically might nonetheless be viewed as having lost ground. Also, given the unlikely prospects of advancement in low-paying jobs and the relatively low levels of economic well-being of black males (Edin and Lein, 1997; Wilson, 1996), the future of many young black women and their families appears dire.

Factors correlated with economic well-being further elucidated the plight of black women, but nonetheless suggested a less dire forecast than that portended in the preceding paragraph. For the entire cohort, work effort and educational level accounted for the greatest variance in the income-to-poverty ratio beyond that accounted for by other correlates in 1987 and 1993. In general, when controlling for such factors as marital status, residence, and self-esteem, among others, those who worked more and had achieved higher levels of education were situated in families whose levels of economic well-being were higher than those who worked less or had less educational achievements. In 1987 and 1993, many in the cohort had worked less than they did in 1986 and 1992 respectively but were nonetheless situated in families with greater economic well-being.

In 1987, black women were among those, along with white males and females, who lived in families with greater levels of economic well-being despite a reduction in their own work effort from that in 1986. Like white males and females, black women who decreased their family size between 1986 and 1987 also experienced greater economic well-being than those whose family size remained the same or increased. In 1993, however, white women were the only ones to work less than they did in 1992 but nonetheless lived in families with greater economic well-being. Although black women whose family size decreased between 1992 and 1993 were more likely to experience greater economic well-being than those whose families did not, they no longer found themselves in circumstances of improved economic well-being and less work effort. Black women did benefit from lower unemployment rates in 1987, but not in 1993. In the mid-1980s, the economy was still expanding, with the gross domestic product (GDP) increasing by more than six percentage points from one year to the next; whereas in the early 1990s, GDP increases were generally well below that (Economic Report of the President, 1997). Overall, the brightest glimmer for black women occurred in the midst of the economic expansion of the 1980s, but it was short-lived, having succumbed to the slower growth characteristic of the early 1990s.

Regardless of labor market conditions in 1987 and 1993, however, black women found to have strong beliefs in control of their lives through self-determination lived in families with greater economic well-being than those found more likely to attribute their circumstances to luck or fate. Paradoxically, such strong beliefs about self-determination played a role among those in the cohort who started out with the lowest relative levels of economic well-being and who most consistently gained the least ground throughout the study period. These beliefs about self-determination played no role beyond that of other factors in accounting for economic well-being among any other group, thereby corroborating much previous research demonstrating the importance of socio-demographic factors and labor market conditions (Blank, 1997; Dolinsky, Caputo, and O'Kane, 1989; Duncan, 1984; Danziger and Gottschalk, 1993 and 1995; Gottschalk, McLanahan, and Sandefur, 1994; Karoly, 1993; Levy and Michel, 1991). Given the mythological status of the importance of self-determination, individual initiative, and economic rewards associated with the American Dream, results of this study suggested that other factors are equally if not more highly correlated with economic well-being when controlling for sex and ethnicity/race. Black women, the least privileged group in American society, were the exception to this general finding. In addition to such other factors as work effort, level of education, and being married, having strong beliefs about one's ability to affect one's circumstances through self-determination mattered in regard to the economic well-being among black women. Hence, to the extent sex and ethnicity/race still work against them, black women who maintain strong beliefs about their ability to affect their lives for the better possess a critical attribute when it comes to improving their economic well-being.

While sex and ethnicity/race may have worked against the black women of the cohort, white men by all accounts were the economic winners, despite only a modest upward trend in economic well-being between 1979 and 1993. They began with and retained throughout the entire study period the highest levels of economic well-being. Of all groups in 1993, white men were the only ones for whom being married correlated with lower levels of economic well-being than being unmarried. This finding was in part a function of the greater proportion of family income attributable to wages and relatively similar or smaller family size of white males in 1993 compared to all other groups. Results in part supported claims that divorce benefited men often at the expense of women and that male economic advantage remained alive and well throughout the 1980s and early 1990s (Coontz, 1997; Rodgers, 1990; Weitzman, 1988).

In the youth cohort studied here, men in general did not necessarily benefit as a group from divorce-related declines in family size. White men did, however, largely because they lived in relatively smaller families to begin with and because their wage-related income exceeded that of most others. Youthful white men seemed to gain their relative advantage from a combination of structural and personal factors as they matured into prime age working adults. Structurally, they reaped greater rewards from the labor market and thereby contributed substantially to total family income which minimized the loss of income due to reduced family size regardless of reason. In the personal realm, white men presumably elected to live in smaller families, relative to others, which enable their higher wage-related contribution to total family income to result in even greater levels of economic well-being when family size decreases.

This combination of structural and personal factors that enhanced the privileged status of white males suggests two different overall strategies to level the economic playing field. Some prefer to look toward labor market strategies comprising, for example, ways to increase the human capital of others so other men and women can better compete with white men or to ensure comparable access to higher paying jobs through affirmative action and the like. Yet others may prefer family-related strategies that encourage white men to emulate other men and women by having larger families or, conversely, to encourage other men and women to emulate white men by living in smaller families.

Several other findings are worth a brief discussion at this point in light of portended implications for the next chapter on economic mobility and the final chapter on policy implications. First, to the extent mothers' education levels reflected a broad array of socio-economic factors influencing the life chances of youthful respondents, these factors receded in importance in regard to economic well-being as the cohort matured. Quite pronounced in 1980, mothers' educational level and all that it represented accounted for no variance in economic well-being in 1993 either in the aggregate nor by sex and ethnicity/race. At issue here is the extent to which early background factors set a trajectory for economic well-being. That is, how might early background factors affect the heights or depths of economic mobility as the cohort moved into its prime working years? Second, to what extent might human capital variables such as education and work effort, both positively correlated with economic well-being in 1987 and 1993 for all sex and ethnicity/race groups, affect the heights or depths of economic mobility controlling for the early background factor of mothers' educational levels and all they represent? This question takes on added importance in light of the emphasis given to human capital and labor market strategies aimed to reduce poverty and raise living standards in an increasingly global economy (Gueron, 1996; Kelso, 1994; Madrick, 1995; Mead, 1996; Murnane and Levy, 1996; Nightingale and Havemen, 1995; Simms, 1996).

Third, findings about the correlation of the other background variables, namely residence (R SMSA) and the rate of unemployment in the area of residence (UNEMP R), are also germane to the next chapter on economic mobility and the final chapter on policy implications. When residence mattered, it did so only for white males and females. Essentially, white males and females who lived within Standard Metropolitan Statistical Areas (SMSAs) lived in families with greater levels of economic well-being than those who did not.

Since work effort was controlled for, this was due in part to higher rates of hourly pay white males and females who resided within SMSAs were able to command. Areas outside SMSAs are primarily rural and the lower rates of hourly pay reflect the greater difficulty such areas have paying the higher wages white males and females can command in more affluent within SMSA areas. In a sharp break from the past when many black Americans sought greater economic advantage by migrating from the more rural South to more urban areas in the North (Mowry and Brownell, 1981), findings of this study suggested that in the 1980s and early 1990s, changing residence from outside to within SMSAs may improve the prospects of upward economic mobility for young white males and females, but have little effect for others.

The unemployment rate in area of residence (UNEMP R) explained much less variance in economic well-being than expected. While the cohort was still youthful, only Hispanic women lived in families that benefited from lower unemployment rates. In the middle of the study period, namely 1987 when economic expansion was reaching its heights, black women and Hispanic men and women lived in families that so benefited. On the whole, their rates of unemployment varied little from one another and were about half the 6.2% reported for the country as a whole (Economic Report, 1997). By 1993, when the unemployment rates for the sex and ethnicity/race groups were about the same as those in 1987 and that of the country was 6.9%, other factors accounted for the variance in economic well-being and eclipsed the unemployment rate in the area of residence as a contributing factor for all groups. To the extent the structural factor of unemployment is less related to the economic well-being of the cohort in its early prime working years, its role in economic mobility may also be eclipsed by other factors. At issue is the extent to which other factors may be within their control so that appropriate strategies can be devised to buffer the effects of downward mobility and to increase the likelihood of upward mobility.

Fourth and finally, findings related to the psychological variable self-esteem are also germane to the next chapter on economic mobility and the final chapter on policy implications. Many economists (e.g., Blank, 1997; Levy and Michel, 1991) focused exclusively on socio-demographic characteristics of individual workers or families, while others who took psychological and attitudinal attributes into account (e.g., Caputo, 1997; Dolinsky, Caputo, and O'Kane, 1989; Duncan 1984; Danziger and Gottschalk, 1993 and 1995; Gottschalk, McLanahan, and Sandefur, 1994) found that they had little or no correlation with economic well-being. In regard to self-esteem, results presented in this chapter generally supported previous studies. For the most part, when self-esteem accounted for variance in economic well-being, it did so in the least amounts both in the aggregate and by sex and ethnicity/race. Nonetheless, it would be mistaken to dismiss self-esteem as an important correlate of economic well-being as some social scientists (e.g., Coontz, 1997) suggest when discussion attempts to prevent or minimize the adverse effects of poverty.

At issue, in part, is to identify those for whom addressing self-esteem might be an appropriate empowering strategy enabling individuals to position themselves in economically more advantageous circumstances than might be possible otherwise. At issue also in part is to determine how much weight to place on enhancing self-esteem given the greater amounts of variance in economic well-being associated with socio-demographic characteristics and labor market conditions. Findings of this chapter suggested that efforts to increase self-esteem might enhance the prospects of upward economic mobility for white males and females, as well as Hispanic females, but would be of little or no related value to black males and females and Hispanic males. To the extent this is the case, many initiatives directed at black women to raise self-esteem as a means to become self-sufficient and escape poverty may be on less solid footing than is otherwise believed (Franklin, 1997).

Chapter 3
ECONOMIC MOBILITY

Introduction

Having assessed income inequality and economic well-being within the youth cohort, the focus now shifts to economic mobility. This chapter examines the nature and extent of economic mobility within the youth cohort between 1979 and 1993. It uses previously introduced measures such as class (adding middle class families to those of affluent and poor) and the income-to-poverty ratio (IPR), and adds new measures such as economic level (EL) signified by decile rankings based on the IPR. As was the case in Chapters 1 and 2, this chapter seeks to shed insight on how well this nationally representative group of maturing respondents fared throughout the 1980s and early 1990s, particularly in regard to differences by sex and ethnicity/race.

The focus on economic mobility reflects concerns of Kelso (1994), who has summarized much of the contemporary debate about poverty, and Blank (1997 and 1995) who has assessed labor market conditions and prospects for low-wage entry jobs, among others (e.g., Danziger, Sandefur, and Weinberg, 1994; Darby, 1996; McFate, Lawson, and Wilson, 1995). Kelso, asking if a war against poverty was really feasible, responded in a "yes, but" manner. Advancing the arguments of the political right that advocates market-like incentives to promote self-reliance, Kelso stressed the importance of identifying factors associated with economic mobility and taking commensurate measures to ensure that disproportionately disadvantaged groups such as single working mothers and black urban males are provided with the requisite means to achieve greater levels of economic well-being and, by extension, to minimize the adverse effects of downward mobility.

As noted previously, researchers have demonstrated that labor-market conditions, demographic factors, family structure, and ethnicity/race affected income dynamics and that psychological and personality-related attributes of individuals had little if any effect (Blank, 1997; Duncan 1984; Danziger and Gottschalk, 1993 and 1995; Karoly, 1993; Levy and Michel, 1991). In addition, in a study of families' earning capacities to escape poverty conducted between 1973 and 1988, Haveman and Buron (1993) reported that (1) groups that were economically secure traditionally, such as white males and females, intact families, and those with relatively high education levels, experienced greater increases in earning capacity poverty (that is, though poor, they tended to generate more income) than did more vulnerable groups such as female-headed families and black female-headed families with children, and (2) the continuing growth in the number of working wives offset increases in earning capacity poverty among intact families.

In two previous studies that relied on the same NLSY data files used in the present study, I found that socio-demographic factors were far more influential than psychological attributes in escaping and entering poverty between 1991 and 1992 (Caputo, 1997a and 1999). In those studies, as noted previously, I incorporated several cumulative variables, such as the number of years in poverty, and change variables, such as change in the number of hours worked between 1991 and 1992. The cumulative variables proved highly predictive of poverty dynamics, eclipsing even human capital variables such as education level. The first of these two studies found that the number of years respondents lived in poverty was the best predictor of escaping poverty, while the number of years respondents made use of public assistance programs was the best predictor of becoming self-sufficient. In both instances, the relationship was inverse, that is, the less time spent in poverty, the greater likelihood of escaping poverty; likewise, the less time on public assistance, the greater the prospect of achieving self-sufficiency. In addition, marital status and change in the number of hours worked between 1991 and 1992 influenced the prospect for escaping poverty, though not for becoming self-sufficient. Likewise, the second study found that the number of years respondents lived in poverty was the best predictor of moving from above poverty in one year to below poverty the following year, while the number of years respondents lived in families that received public assistance was the best predictor of moving from self-support to entering into a public assistance program from one year to the next.

This chapter extends my earlier work using this youth cohort to identify factors associated with entering and escaping poverty in several ways. First, as in Chapters 1 and 2, Chapter 3 takes greater advantage of the longitudinal nature of the NLSY data files and uses time-series analysis to examine secular trends in economic mobility in the youth cohort stratified by sex and ethnicity/race. As noted previously, because of its ability to detect autocorrelation, time-series analysis allows for a more accurate reflection of trends than do other time dimension portraits often presented in cross-sectional and other long-term studies (Rubin and Babbie, 1997; Webster, 1992).

Second, rather than focus exclusively on entering and escaping poverty, this chapter examines economic mobility throughout the economic spectrum. In doing so, it incorporates both absolute and relative measures of economic well-being, such as the income-to-poverty ratio (IPR) and related decile rankings respectively. Use of such measures enables a determination of the extent to which families of varying degrees of economic well-being gained or lost economic standing, both on a year-to-year basis and over the entire 15-year span of the study period.

Third, this chapter identifies demographic, human capital, and psychological correlates associated with a cumulative measure of economic mobility, namely the average lifetime change in annual economic levels between 1979 and 1993. It makes greater use of cumulative variables, such as the number of years respondents were married, were employed as a full-time worker, and received public assistance. The chapter rests on the assumption that economic mobility is better understood as part of a longitudinal or secular process rather than as a single, one-time event. From this understanding the merits of policies and programs aimed to enhance the prospects of upward mobility and minimize the degree of downward mobility can be better assessed. Chapter 3 addresses the following questions in regard to the youth cohort as it matured throughout the 1980s and early 1990s:

1. To what extent did economic mobility among families increase or decrease?
2. What were the levels and trends of economic well-being among families in the lowest and highest economic levels?
3. What was the relationship between class, based, as it was, on the objective or absolute components of family size and income of the poverty thresholds, and economic mobility, based, as it was, on a family's relative economic position or level inherent to decile rankings?
4. To what extent did lifetime changes in economic levels vary by

sex and ethnicity/race?

5. What human capital, demographic, and psychological characteristics were correlated with lifetime economic mobility?
6. How did significant correlates of lifetime economic mobility vary by sex and ethnicity/race?

Measures

Respondents were stratified by both absolute and relative measures related to total family income. As in previous chapters, the absolute measure, class, refers to a family's economic standing in relation to official poverty thresholds in any given year and as such it accounts for family size. For purposes of this chapter, respondents fell into one of three classes: poor (PC), middle (MC), or affluent (AC). As in previous chapters, poor respondents were those whose family income fell below the official poverty thresholds and affluent respondents were those whose family income exceeded seven times those thresholds. Respondents whose family incomes fell between poor and affluent were classified as middle class.

In addition, the measure economic level (EL) reflected the relative economic standing of a respondent's family. To obtain EL, respondents' income-to-poverty ratios (IPRs) were rank ordered annually by deciles. To determine the extent of economic mobility (EM), a respondent's EL in one year was subtracted from the previous year's, which, because it was based on IPR decile rankings, accounted for total family income and family size. Annual EM changes were then summed over the entire study period and divided by 15 to determine the net economic mobility or Average Lifetime Change in Economic Level (ALCEL) of respondents.

Table 3.1 summarizes the variables used in this chapter.

Table 3.1 *Descriptors and Correlates of Economic Mobility*

DESCRIPTORS:

AC	Affluent Class: family income at least seven times the poverty status (1=yes)
ALCEL	Average lifetime change in economic level between 1979 and 1993
EL	Economic level signified by decile ranking based on family income
EM	Economic mobility measured as the change in decile ranking based on family income from one year to the next
ETHNICITY/ RACE	Black, White, Hispanic (non-white, non-black)
IPR	Income-to-Poverty Ratio, the measure of economic well-being
MC	Middle Class: family income between poverty and affluent classes
PC	Poverty Class: family income at or below the official poverty thresholds
SEX	Female, Male
YEAR	1979-1993

CORRELATES:

BACKGROUND VARIABLES:

AAUP	Average annual unemployment rate in area of residence

Table 3.1 *Descriptors and Correlates of Economic Mobility continued*

AGE R	Age of respondent
HGC R	Highest grade completed, respondent
HGC RM	Highest grade completed, respondent's mother
CUMULATIVE VARIABLES:	
YAFDC	Years received any Aid to Families with Dependent Children benefits
YFS	Years received any Food Stamps
YFTWK	Years employed as a full-time worker
YMS	Years married
YSSI	Years received any Supplemental Security Income benefits
YUC	Years received any Unemployment Compensation benefits
PSYCHOLOGICAL VARIABLES:	
LOC	Internal-external locus of control as determined by the scale developed by Rotter
SELF EST	Self-esteem scores as measured by the Rosenberg self-esteem scale

Seven variables used as descriptors and correlates of economic well-being in Chapter 2 are also used here, including the background variables age of respondent, ethnicity/race, highest grade completed of respondent, highest grade completed of respondent's mother, and sex, and the psychological variables internal-external locus of control and self-esteem. Since the criterion variable in this chapter constitutes the net change in economic mobility between 1979 and 1993 (ALCEL), the variable average annual unemployment rate in area of residence (AAUP) was also used as a background correlate. In addition, six cumulative event variables were examined to assess the direction and strength of their relationship with net economic mobility or ALCEL. These variables included the number of years respondents were married (YMS), had full-time employment (YFTWK), and received any benefits from Aid to Families with Dependent Children (YAFDC), Food Stamps (YFS), Supplemental Security Income (YSSI), or Unemployment Compensation (YUC).

The addition of these cumulative event variables afforded an opportunity to assess their relative contribution, beyond that of other background and psychological characteristics, to account for variance in ALCEL. To the extent that these cumulative event variables correlated with the economic mobility of respondents over the course of their maturing years, policy makers and others can better assess the merits of preventive strategies designed to increase the prospects of escaping poverty and of buffering downward mobility earlier rather than later in the life cycle. For example, to the extent the use of public benefits over time had little or no relation with economic mobility over the fifteen years of this study period, regardless of direction, then fears of "dependency" on government assistance in times of need may be less a cause of concern than many contemporary policy makers suggest (e.g., Armey, 1995; Gingrich, 1995).

In light of findings from previous research and Chapters 1 and 2 in regard to their relative advantage, white men were expected to exhibit the greatest upward mobility and the least downward mobility, despite their initial high level of economic well-being, between 1979 and 1993. Because black women lived in the most economically disadvantaged of all sex and ethnicity/race groups, their families were expected to have the lowest levels of upward mobility. In addition, the families of more affluent black women were nonetheless expected to exhibit the steepest downward mobility.

Among the background variables, highest grade completed of respondents (HGC R) was thought to account for the greatest variance in Average Lifetime Change in Economic Level (ALCEL). Families with respondents of higher levels of completed education were expected to demonstrate either greater net upward economic mobility or less downward mobility than those with lower levels of completed education. Among the psychological variables, internal-external locus of control (LOC) was thought to be correlated with ALCEL for black women; self-esteem (SELF EST), for white men and women. Although being married was found in many previous studies to be correlated with economic well-being in general for any given year, the number of years married (YMS) was nonetheless thought to be inversely related with ALCEL. That is, to the extent longer marriages signified stability or had a "settling in effect," then family income was also thought to be associated with less dramatic changes in economic mobility over time. Likewise, the number of years respondents were employed in full-time work (YFTWK) was thought to be inversely related to ALCEL. Part-time and contingency workers were thought to have far greater variations in annual hours worked and income than full-time workers (Tilly, 1996). Like length of marriage, increased time spent in full-time employment signified stability or steadiness, resulting over time in less pronounced shifts in economic mobility.

The inclusion of number of years families received Aid to Families with Dependent Children (YAFDC), Food Stamps (YFS), Supplemental Security Income (YSSI), and Unemployment Compensation (YUC) benefits among the cumulative variables reflects the contemporary preoccupation with the role of public assistance programs with economic well-being (Blank, 1997; Burton, 1992; Caputo, 1997a, 1997b and 1999; Duncan, et al., 1995; Edin and Lein, 1997; Jencks, 1996; Kelso, 1994; Loury, 1996; Murray, 1996). Three of the four benefits examined here are cash. In the short run, cash benefits such as SSI and UC might contribute to upward mobility or minimize the effect of downward mobility, albeit in a limited sense. Over an extended period of time, however, increased use of such benefits was thought to signify more stable, albeit relatively low, levels of economic well-being. Although the receipt of Food Stamps would not contribute directly to economic well-being as measured for purposes of this study, its continued use was also thought to reflect stable but relatively low levels of economic well-being. Hence, to the extent that families received benefits from any of these programs, it was thought that the respective length of time would be inversely related to the measure of net economic mobility, Average Lifetime Change in Economic Level (ALCEL).

Procedures

To determine the extent of economic mobility (EM), a respondent's economic level (EL)-that is, decile ranking-in one year was first subtracted from that in the preceding year. This procedure resulted in the distribution of respondents who demonstrated either upward (in varying degrees, from 1 to 9), downward (also in varying degrees, from -1 to -9), or no relative economic mobility (0) from one year to the next. Second, this tripartite distribution based on the relative EL or decile ranking measure was then stratified by the absolute tripartite variable class, also by year. This procedure produced annual percentage distributions of poor, middle, and affluent families which demonstrated either upward, downward, or no relative economic mobility (EM) from the preceding year. Time series analysis was used to determine the secular trend in the proportion of families which demonstrated upward, downward, or no EM by year and class. To assess the presence of autocorrelation and, hence, the reliability of the simple regression model, the Durban-Watson Statistic (*d*) is reported in addition to the coefficient of determination (r^2) and the regression coefficient (*b*). Third, to determine if the average lifetime change in economic level (ALCEL) differed among sex and ethnicity/race groups, the general linear model (GLM) procedure was conducted separately on each 1979 decile ranking. When appropriate for post hoc analysis of ALCEL between pairs of the six sex and ethnicity/race groups, the LSMEANS procedure was used. The F ratio, follow-up pairwise comparisons, and results of their respective tests of statistical significance are reported.

Finally, multiple regression analysis was used to determine correlates of the average change in economic levels or net economic mobility (ALCEL) between 1979 and 1993. For this procedure, the twelve correlates in Table 3.1 were regressed on ALCEL. Correlates comprised four background, six cumulative, and two psychological variables. ALCEL values ranged from -9 to +9. To indicate how much the ALCEL would change for every 1-unit change in each of the respective correlates, I reported the multiple regression coefficient (*b*) and the accompanying *t test* for statistical significance. For the correlates found to be significant, I also reported the uniqueness indices (UI) and accompanying F value that tested the statistical significance of each uniqueness index. The UI signified the percentage of variance in the average lifetime change in economic level (ALCEL) accounted for by a given correlate beyond the variance accounted for by the other eleven in the model (Hatcher and Stepanski, 1994).

Results

Trends in Economic Mobility. Table 3.2 shows the percentage distribution of economic mobility (EM) by Class and Year. Most notable are the increasing proportions of respondents who lived in families whose economic level (EL) or decile ranking remained relatively stable, regardless of class. Figure 3.1 (see page 159) highlights the trends in the percentage distribution of poor, middle, and affluent families whose EL had not changed from the previous year.

Between 1979 and 1993, the trend in percent distributions of those demonstrating no change in economic level (EL), that is, in their relative decile ranking, was strongly positive for poor, middle class, and affluent families. As Table 3.2 and Figure 3.1 show, 26.6% of poor families (PC), 21.5% of middle class families (MC), and 46.4% of affluent families (AC) demonstrated no change in their respective EL in 1980 from that in 1979, whereas 59.7%, 36.9%, and 66.4% respectively showed no change in 1993 from that in 1992. These results suggested a hardening of the economic arteries, so to speak, an "econosclerosis," signifying an increasingly impermeable boundary within which a family's relative economic standing stabilized as this cohort of youth matured. Econosclerosis was most severe for poor families which demonstrated a 124% increase of those with no change in EL between 1980 and 1993, followed by middle class families which demonstrated a 72% increase, and by affluent families, a 42% increase.

The increasing percentages of families demonstrating no change in economic level (EL) or decile ranking between 1979 and 1993 were accompanied by declining percentages of poor families demonstrating downward mobility and affluent families demonstrating upward mobility. Among poor families in 1980, 67.9% declined in relative economic standing from that of 1979, whereas in 1993, 40.3% of them did from that of 1992. It should be noted, however, that among poor families, the lowest percentage of downward mobility occurred in 1988 from that of 1987 (38.8%), with moderately higher percentages afterwards, albeit still well below the 67.9% of 1980. Among affluent families in 1980, 53.6% had increased in relative economic standing from that of 1979, whereas in 1993, 33.6% did from that of 1992. These results indicated that on one hand fewer non-poor families became poor as the cohort matured, while on the other hand fewer non-affluent families became affluent. Given the increased percentages of families demonstrating no change in economic level (EL) by Class between 1979 and 1993, these results portend to the increased intractability of poverty for those fewer families likely to become poor and to the increased likelihood of remaining affluent for those fewer non-affluent families fortunate enough to enter that class.

Increasing percentages of families demonstrating no change in economic level (EL) were also accompanied by declining percentages of poor class families (PC) demonstrating upward economic mobility through 1986 and none thereafter, and virtually no downward mobility of affluent class families (AC). Among the PC in 1980, 5.5% increased in relative economic standing from that of 1979, whereas in 1986, 1.2% of them did from that of 1985. Between 1987 and 1993, poor families who remained poor from one year to the next experienced no upward mobility. Two factors may account for this result. On one hand, the lowest percentile of the family income distribution may have captured all poor families such that after 1986 no families whose income fell below the poverty thresholds appeared in the second decile. If this were the case, then poor families who demonstrated upward economic mobility from one year to the next escaped poverty. On the other hand, the income-to-poverty ratio (IPR) among the poor may have increased in absolute terms, such that the economic well-being of the poorest poor got increasingly higher over time and that any upward mobility would result in escaping poverty. As Figure 3.2 (see page 160) shows, both factors came into play.

Table 3.2 *Percent*[1] *Distribution of Economic Mobility, 1980-1993, by Class and Year, Income-to-Poverty Ratio Decile Change (n=2745)*

	Class								
	Poor			Middle			Affluent		
Year	Downward	No Change	Upward	Downward	No Change	Upward	Downward	No Change	Upward
1980	67.9	26.6	5.5	35.7	21.5	42.8		46.4	53.6
1981	67.7	28.3	4.0	37.5	21.6	40.9		39.6	60.4
1982	57.4	35.5	7.1	32.3	24.2	43.5		38.8	61.2
1983	54.7	40.4	4.8	35.8	25.3	38.9		41.2	58.8
1984	57.5	39.5	3.1	37.1	26.6	36.3		43.1	56.9
1985	51.3	46.5	2.2	35.7	27.3	37.0		49.2	50.8
1986	53.0	45.8	1.2	36.3	26.0	37.7		40.1	59.9
1987	48.7	51.3		36.4	28.3	35.3		53.9	46.1
1988	38.8	61.2		37.3	31.5	31.2		62.0	38.0
1989	45.3	54.7		34.3	31.9	33.8	3.8	53.7	42.5
1990	45.9	54.1		31.5	33.6	34.8	1.7	64.5	33.8
1991	37.1	62.9		30.8	35.9	33.4		65.2	34.8
1992	43.5	56.5		31.0	38.1	30.9		65.6	34.4
1993	40.3	59.7		33.2	36.9	30.0		66.4	33.6

[1] Weighted by year. Due to rounding, percents may not add to 100.

In 1987 the income-to-poverty ratio's (IPR) upper limit for the lowest economic level (EL), that is, the first decile ranking, was 1.09, exceeding the poverty threshold of 1.00 for the first time and remaining above it through 1993. After 1986, the lowest EL included both poor and non-poor families. Hence, it would be possible for some non-poor families to experience downward mobility into the lowest EL without becoming poor. Concomitantly, although fewer in number, poor families who demonstrated upward economic mobility were increasingly likely to escape poverty even though they may have remained in the lowest EL, albeit close to the IPR's upper limit among poor families in any given year. In addition, the average annual IPR among the lowest EL families increased from .50 between 1979 and 1986 to .65 between 1987 and 1993. These results corroborated the improved economic well-being of the poor found in Chapter 2. They signified that, although poor families were increasingly likely to remain poor, they were likely to do so at a higher level of economic well-being than in earlier years.

On the whole, results were mixed regarding the relationship between economic mobility and poverty as the cohort matured. On the one hand, those who became poor were increasingly likely over time to remain so. On the other hand, the declining numbers of families fortunate enough to increase their relative economic standing by one level had increased chances of escaping poverty, while those less fortunate who remained in poverty were nonetheless likely to do so at a higher level of economic well-being than was the case during the cohort's younger years.

Results were also mixed regarding the relationship between economic mobility and affluence. As was the case among poor families, the incidence of affluent families demonstrating no change in economic level (EL) from one year to the next increased as the cohort matured. While the percentage of respondents who lived in non-poor families which became poor declined over time, the percentage of those in non-affluent families which became affluent also declined. With the exceptions of 1989 and 1990, it was not possible for respondents living in affluent families to demonstrate upward mobility from within the top EL because the income-to-poverty ratio's (IPR's) lower limit of top decile ranking families did not exceed seven times the poverty thresholds. Given the increased percentage of respondents living in affluent families likely to remain so over time, fewer respondents were likely to become part of affluent families even though they may have moved into the top EL from a lower level in the preceding year. Nonetheless, as was the case with respondents living in poor families, those in the fewer families likely to move into the affluent class (AC) did so at a higher level of affluence after 1986. As Figure 3.3 (see page 161) illustrates, between 1979 and 1986, the top EL had an average annual IPR of 8.08, whereas between 1987 and 1993, the average annual IPR was 9.17.

Table 3.3 *Percent [1] Distribution of Economic Mobility, 1980-1993, by Class, Income-to-Poverty Ratio Decile Change, and Year*

	Poor																		
	IPR Decile Change																		
Year	-9	-8	-7	-6	-5	-4	-3	-2	-1	0	1	2	3	4	5	6	7	8	9
1980	4.7	4.5	5.4	7.6	6.8	4.7	9.8	11.5	12.9	26.6	5.5								
1981	3.6	8.7	4.4	4.4	5.2	6.4	7.6	09.2	17.9	28.3	4.0								
1982	5.7	5.8	4.9	3.5	3.5	6.1	6.0	09.6	12.4	35.5	7.1								
1983	2.7	4.5	2.8	3.0	4.9	7.4	6.0	08.2	15.2	40.4	4.8								
1984	2.3	3.0	3.2	2.5	3.5	8.1	7.7	08.5	18.7	39.5	3.1								
1985	3.6	1.3	2.7	1.9	5.2	3.2	7.3	07.9	18.2	46.5	2.2								
1986	4.8	0.9	2.5	2.9	5.2	0.9	4.9	11.6	19.2	45.8	1.2								
1987	1.1	0.7	4.3	4.0	3.7	3.0	5.1	09.1	17.5	51.3									
1988		1.8	2.3	1.9	1.8	2.8	5.0	04.9	18.4	61.2									
1989	1.3	0.9	4.0	5.8	4.9	1.7	5.4	06.9	14.4	54.7									
1990	1.0	3.8	1.9	2.6	3.5	3.3	2.4	11.5	16.0	54.1									
1991	1.0	0.7	0.2	2.0	4.8	4.8	2.8	07.5	16.7	62.9									
1992	0.9	0.7	2.7	0.7	2.9	4.2	7.4	07.6	16.3	56.5									
1993		1.8	2.6	1.0	0.8	5.7	8.3	07.1	13.0	59.7									

Table 3.3 *Percent [1] Distribution of Economic Mobility, 1980-1993, by Class, Income-to-Poverty Ratio Decile Change, and Year continued*

	Middle																		
	IPR Decile Change																		
Year	-9	-8	-7	-6	-5	-4	-3	-2	-1	0	1	2	3	4	5	6	7	8	9
1980		0.4	1.0	1.6	2.7	3.1	5.4	7.5	14.0	21.5	14.5	10.8	5.9	4.2	2.8	1.9	1.2	1.0	0.6
1981		0.7	1.0	1.5	2.9	3.9	5.0	7.9	14.6	21.6	14.2	09.9	5.7	3.4	2.8	2.0	1.3	0.8	0.7
1982		0.3	0.7	1.8	2.0	4.3	4.6	6.6	12.0	24.2	17.2	10.1	5.9	4.0	2.6	1.8	1.0	0.6	0.2
1983		0.4	0.7	1.3	2.9	2.8	4.3	7.0	16.3	25.3	15.5	08.8	4.9	3.3	2.7	1.5	1.2	0.7	0.2
1984		0.6	1.2	1.0	1.6	3.4	4.4	9.0	15.8	26.6	13.2	08.7	4.7	3.2	2.3	1.7	1.2	1.0	0.2
1985		0.2	0.6	1.4	2.0	3.0	4.5	6.6	17.4	27.3	16.5	08.2	4.9	2.9	2.3	1.0	0.5	0.6	
1986		0.4	0.6	1.2	1.8	3.4	5.2	7.8	16.0	26.0	18.8	07.4	3.7	2.7	1.8	1.6	1.2	0.4	
1987	0.1	0.3	0.8	1.4	1.8	4.2	4.1	6.6	17.3	28.3	16.2	07.7	4.3	2.6	2.1	1.2	0.4	0.8	
1988		0.2	0.5	0.8	1.7	3.0	3.5	8.6	18.9	31.5	14.2	06.4	4.0	2.7	2.2	0.6	0.6	0.4	0.1
1989		0.1	0.6	0.8	1.4	1.8	4.1	7.8	18.1	31.9	17.6	07.7	4.1	1.8	1.1	0.7	0.7	0.2	
1990		0.3	0.2	0.4	1.6	2.1	3.4	6.0	17.5	33.6	18.9	07.4	4.1	1.9	1.1	0.5	0.5	0.3	
1991		0.1	0.6	0.5	1.3	1.4	3.0	6.4	17.4	35.9	19.4	05.8	3.1	2.5	1.2	1.0	0.3	0.1	
1992		0.1	0.4	0.4	1.4	2.2	3.7	6.1	16.7	38.1	17.4	05.8	2.7	2.0	1.4	0.8	0.6	0.3	
1993			0.4	0.8	2.0	1.7	3.0	6.7	18.5	36.9	14.8	05.7	3.0	2.5	1.8	1.1	0.8	0.4	

Table 3.3 *Percent [1] Distribution of Economic Mobility, 1980-1993, by Class, Income-to-Poverty Ratio Decile Change, and Year continued*

Affluent

IPR Decile Change

Year	-9	-8	-7	-6	-5	-4	-3	-2	-1	0	1	2	3	4	5	6	7	8	9
1980										46.4	09.3	04.7	11.8	6.3	4.2	1.5	3.7	5.8	6.3
1981										39.6	10.6	05.4	06.7	4.0	6.6	8.0	3.4	6.5	9.2
1982										38.8	12.6	01.9	05.9	7.5	8.2	3.1	7.0	7.8	7.3
1983										41.2	10.6	05.8	05.7	6.2	3.0	5.2	9.0	9.0	4.4
1984										43.1	15.3	10.6	05.8	3.9	6.3	4.7	5.7	2.0	2.7
1985										49.2	10.9	11.5	06.7	4.8	1.9	1.8	4.8	4.9	3.4
1986										40.1	25.2	07.1	07.8	3.1	3.5	3.7	3.3	2.8	3.6
1987										53.9	15.2	05.4	05.7	3.1	4.8	4.9	1.9	2.9	2.1
1988										62.0	11.5	06.0	01.2	5.1	4.2	4.3	2.3	1.1	2.3
1989									3.8	53.7	18.1	06.7	05.4	5.2	1.5	2.5	1.7	1.7	0.3
1990									1.7	64.5	15.8	08.9	04.4	1.0	2.1	0.6	0.3	0.5	0.1
1991										65.2	16.8	08.9	01.8	3.9	1.8	0.6			1.0
1992										65.6	19.1	06.4	02.1	2.3	2.3		2.3	0.4	2.4
1993										66.4	12.8	08.8	01.6	3.9	0.8	1.2	1.1	0.8	2.6

[1] Weighted by year. Due to rounding, percents may not add to 100.

It should be noted, however, that after 1989 the income-to-poverty ratio's (IPR's) lower limit trend is downward, such that by 1991 upwardly mobile non-affluent families could move into the top economic level (EL) without becoming affluent, much as they could prior to 1989. And in 1989 and 1990, affluent families could be found in the top two ELs, signifying that only affluent families occupied the top tier. As a result, relatively small percentages of affluent families who remained affluent nonetheless demonstrated downward mobility in 1989 (3.8%) and 1990 (1.7%). These results suggested that throughout the 1980s and early 1990s, increasingly more families became affluent such that in 1989 and 1990 they occupied the entire top or tenth EL and a portion of the ninth decile. The increased entry of respondents into the affluent class (AC), however, was short-lived. By 1991, upwardly mobile respondents living in non-affluent families could become part of the top EL and still have IPRs below the 7.00 threshold level of the AC. Nonetheless, like their counterparts who entered the poor class (PC), the fewer respondents living in families which entered the AC were increasingly likely to remain there and they did so at a higher level of economic well-being than in the earlier years of the study period.

For the most part, the trends in the percentage distributions of changes in economic level (EL) or decile ranking by class suggested that economic mobility became increasingly restricted for this cohort of youth between 1979 and 1993. Nonetheless, there was much mobility. Table 3.3 shows the percent distributions of economic mobility by actual changes in decile rankings over the study period and highlights the annual movement of poor (PC) and middle (MC) class, as well as affluent (AC) families.

Respondents who lived in families that became poor (PC) in any given year arrived there from all along the economic spectrum of the previous year. The greatest percentages of those who became poor in any given year, however, came primarily from those closest to poverty, namely those whose economic level (EL) dropped one, two, or three deciles. And only in the earlier years did more than 10% of respondents living in poor families come from the ranks furthest from poverty, namely those whose EL dropped seven or more deciles. As noted above, in the early 1980s, some in the PC in any given year were also poor in the previous year, but nonetheless experienced upward mobility insufficient to lift them above the poverty line. After 1986, however, because of the rising standard of living, as indexed by the upward trend of the income-to-poverty ratio, all poor families fell within the first or bottom decile of income distribution.

The middle class (MC), which comprised the second through ninth decile rankings, exhibited a fairly equitable distribution of entrants across economic levels (ELs). As noted, over time an increasingly sizable minority of respondents who lived in MC families had been MC the preceding year. For the most part, respondents who lived in families that entered the MC in any given year were likely to have either gained or lost decile rankings, that is, to have increased or decreased their relative economic level, to a roughly equitable degree. The highest percentages of entrants into the MC in any given year had either increased or decreased one or two decile rankings from the previous year. These results suggested that respondents who had lived in both previously poor and affluent families entered the ranks of the MC in roughly equal proportions throughout the study period.

As was the case with respondents whose families entered the poor class (PC), those whose families ended up affluent (AC) in any given year also arrived there from all along the economic spectrum of the previous year. The greatest percentages of those who became affluent in any given year, however, came primarily from those closest to affluence, namely those whose economic level (EL) increased one, two, or three decile rankings, although after 1987 the annual percentages entering the AC from a jump of three deciles declined by more than half that of previous years. It should also be noted that in the earlier years, notably 1980-1983, sizable percentages of respondents living in non-affluent families entered the AC as a result of extensive increased mobility. In 1983, for example, 9% of respondents living in affluent families had increased seven deciles from their 1982 EL, while another 9% and 4.4% respectively jumped eight and nine levels.

Average Lifetime Change in Economic Level. Between 1979 and 1993, 14.2% of all families reported no change in economic level (EL). Table 3.4 shows the distribution of the Average Lifetime Change in Economic Level (ALCEL) by EL in 1979, sex and ethnicity/race.

Table 3.4 *Average Lifetime Change in Economic Level (ALCEL), by 1979 Economic Level, Sex and Ethnicity/Race*

PANEL A: ALCEL MEANS[1]

Economic Level (Decile Ranking) in 1979

	1	2	3	4	5	6	7	8	9	10	n	(%) [2]
n	392	398	361	283	255	242	207	191	216	200		
Black Males	3.08	1.65	1.44	0.61	-1.05	-1.63	-0.80	-3.61	-2.54	-3.22	326	05.6
White Males	4.14	3.40	2.44	1.59	0.85	0.18	-0.63	-1.75	-2.27	-3.18	663	38.6
Hispanic Males	3.16	2.31	2.50	1.09	-0.23	-0.42	-0.12	-0.63	-2.27	-3.66	178	02.2
Black Females	1.70	0.73	0.17	-0.02	-0.84	-1.75	-3.42	-3.45	-5.13	-4.08	525	08.4
White Females	3.46	2.79	2.25	1.13	0.41	-0.55	-1.36	-2.10	-2.91	-2.7	825	42.5
Hispanic Females	2.71	1.37	1.33	-0.45	-1.16	-1.04	-0.25	-1.80	-1.91	-4.66	228	02.8

PANEL B: RANK ORDER OF MEAN ALCEL DIFFERENCES[3]

		F
1	WM, WF> HM, BM, HF> BF	8.17[a]
2	WM, WF> HM, BM, HF> BF	12.00[a]
3	HM, WM, WF, BM, HF> BF; WM>BM; WM>HF	7.84[a]
4	WM, WF, HM, BM, BF, HF; WM > BF; WM> HF; HM>HF	3.23[b]
5	WM, WF, HM, BM, BF, HF; WM > BF; WM>BM;WM>HF; WF>BF; WF>BM; WF>HF	2.14

Table 3.4 *Average Lifetime Change in Economic Level (ALCEL), by 1979 Economic Level, Sex and Ethnicity/Race continued*

6	WM, HM, WF, HF, BM, BF; WM>WF; WM>BM;WM > BF	2.82[c]
7	HM, HF, WM, BM, WF> BF	2.88[c]
8	HM, WM, HF, WF, BF, BM; HM>BF; HM>BM; WM>BM	2.14
9	HF, HM, WM, BM, WF > BF	3.36[b]
10	WF, WM, BM, HM, BF, HF; WF>HF	1.39

Legend: BM = Black Male, WM = White Male, HM = Hispanic Male, BF = Black Female, WF = White Female, HF = Hispanic Female

[1] Unadjusted means.

[2] Weighted, based on 1994 sampling weight.

[3] Rankings signify the order based on highest absolute adjusted mean values such that when all sex & ethnicity/race groups had a net loss of economic level over the study period, as in the 8th decile ranking of 1979, those with smaller losses were ranked higher than those with greater losses. Pairwise comparisons are significant at the p=.05 level.

[a] $p < .001$; [b] $p < .01$; [c] $p < .05$

◆ Advantage White and Male, Disadvantage Black and Female

As Panel A in Table 3.4 indicates, due in part to their start positions, families in the lowest three economic levels (ELs) in 1979 were on average upwardly mobile, while those in the top four decile rankings lost economic ground regardless of sex and ethnicity/race. As Panel B in Table 3.4 highlights, however, the extent of economic mobility varied considerably by sex and ethnicity/race, for the most part, regardless of initial position. The major exceptions were families in first and second ELs where white males and females had statistically significant greater average upward economic mobility than Hispanic males, black males, and Hispanic females, all of whom in turn had significantly greater upward mobility than black females. Exceptional also were black females who demonstrated the least upward mobility and the most downward mobility relative to other groups. In the third EL, for example, all other groups had greater lifetime upward mobility than did black females to a statistically significant degree, while in the seventh and ninth ELs black females had the greatest downward mobility of all other groups. Finally, although some groups demonstrated roughly comparable lifetime economic mobility regardless of starting position, white males demonstrated the most upward mobility and the least downward mobility relative to some other groups. In the third EL, for example, the upward lifetime economic mobility of white males was virtually indistinguishable from that of Hispanic males and white females, but was greater to a statistically significant degree than that of black males and Hispanic females. In the seventh EL, for another example, the downward mobility of white males was virtually indistinguishable from all other groups except black females who had the greatest decline.

Correlates of Economic Mobility. Table 3.5 shows, for the entire study sample, the correlation matrix, means and standard deviations of net economic mobility, that is, the average lifetime change in economic level (ALCEL), and the twelve correlates used in the multiple regression analysis. Table 3.6 shows, by sex and ethnicity/race, the percent of variance in the ALCELs accounted for by each statistically significant correlate beyond the variance accounted for by the other eleven correlates. The regression coefficients, *b*s, and their corresponding *t* tests of statistical significance appear in table 3.6 for each correlate, while Uniqueness Indices and corresponding F tests appear only for correlates found to be statistically significant.

Table 3.5 *Correlation Matrix, Means and Standard Deviations of Average Lifetime Change in Economic Level (ALCEL) and Correlates*

Correlates	ALCEL	AAUR	AGE R	HGC R	HGC RM	LOCUS
ALCEL	1.000					
AAUR	-.056**	1.000				
AGE R	-.053**	-.008	1.000			
HGC R	.165***	-.055**	.005	1.000		
HGC RM	-.037*	-.098***	-.007	.386***	1.000	
LOCUS	-.016	.030	-.054**	-.128***	-.085***	1.000
SELF EST	.068***	-.031	.076***	.327***	.197***	-.184***
YAFDC	-.104***	.084***	-.037*	-.219***	-.154***	.081***
YFS	-.124***	.108***	-.013	-.306***	-.223***	.097***
YFTWK	.121***	-.096***	.133***	.127***	.121***	-.058**
YM	-.118***	.116***	.176***	-.078***	-.012	-.047*
YSSI	-.052**	.033	-.016	-.143***	-.081***	.071***
YUC	-.060**	.137***	.066***	-.169***	-.079***	.016

*** $p < .001$; ** $p < .01$; * $p < .05$.

Table 3.5 *Correlation Matrix, Means and Standard Deviations of Average Lifetime Change in Economic Level (ALCEL) and Correlates continued*

SELF EST	YAFDC	YFS	YFTWK	YM	YSSI	YUC	MEAN	SD
							0.226	3.351
							3.080	0.689
							32.898	1.553
							12.982	2.384
							10.799	3.150
							11.489	1.539
1.000							32.568	4.121
-.155***	1.000						1.004	2.732
-.208***		1.000					1.628	3.408
.193***	-.407***	-.453***	1.000				6.517	4.160
.072***	-.212***	-.151***	.083***	1.000			6.376	5.214
-.127***	.266***	.416***	-.281***	-.171***	1.000		0.302	1.086
-.044*	-.050**	-.015	.014	.039*	-.046**	1.000	0.925	1.621

Table 3.6 *Regression Correlates of Average Lifetime Change in Economic Level*

	Male											
Correlates	Black				White				Hispanic			
Background Variables:	*b*	t	UI	F	*b*	t	UI	F	*b*	t	UI	F
AAUR	-0.156	-0.477			-0.370	-1.835			-0.408	-1.204		
AGE R	-0.251	-2.076*	.0124	3.981*	0.008	0.086			-0.279	-1.627		
HGC R	0.232	2.358*	.0160	5.371*	0.300	4.435***	.0279	19.244***	0.287	2.442*	.0329	5.962*
HGC RM	-0.185	-2.696**	.0209	6.718**	-0.010	-0.156	-0.133	-2.061*	.0234	4.246*		
Cumulative Variables:												
YAFDC	0.033	0.137			-0.459	-1.804			-0.032	-0.101		
YFS	-0.029	-0.241			0.050	0.373			0.060	0.374		
YFTWK	0.081	1.422			0.079	1.547			0.008	0.103		
YM	0.101	1.422*	.0129	4.137*	-0.095	-2.866**	.0116	8.037**	-0.001	-0.028		
YSSI	-0.065	-0.448			0.658	2.761**	.0108	7.456**	0.151	0.330		

Table 3.6 *Regression Correlates of Average Lifetime Change in Economic Level continued*

YUC	-0.261	-2.387*	.0164	5.265*	0.053	0.716			-0.040	-0.254		
Psychological Variables:												
LOCUS	0.117	0.934			-0.082	-0.934			0.050	0.316		
SELF EST	0.050	1.074			0.010	0.301			0.085	1.311		
n	326				663				178			
R^2	0.0981				0.0770				0.0879			
df	312		312		649		649		164		164	
					Female							
Correlates	Black				White				Hispanic			
Background Variables:												
	b	t	UI	F	*b*	t	UI	F	*b*	t	UI	F
AAUR	0.152	0.683			-0.053	-0.326			0.260	0.949		
AGE R		-0.093	-1.172			-0.108	-1.429			-0.087	-0.665	

Table 3.6 *Regression Correlates of Average Lifetime Change in Economic Level continued*

HGC R	0.146	2.064*	.0072	4.259*	0.227	3.759***	.0141	12.247***	0.190	2.249*	.0202	5.059*
HGC RM	-0.173	-3.494***	.0207	12.208***	-0.141	-2.700**	.0082	7.173**	-0.083	-1.487		
Cumulative Variables:												
YAFDC	0.034	0.681			-0.085	-0.897			0.014	0.135		
YFS	-0.094	-1.997*	.0067	3.988*	-0.010	-0.122			-0.037	-0.457		
YFTWK	0.163	3.844***	.0251	14.779***	0.134	3.936***	.0175	15.241***	0.067	1.006		
YM	-0.037	-1.305			-0.067	-2.471*	.0069	6.007*	-0.054	-1.257		
YSSI	-0.006	-0.069			-0.189	-1.152			-0.216	-1.230		
YUC	-0.127	-1.274			0.034	0.373			-0.276	-2.206*	.0195	4.866*
Psychological Variables:												
LOCUS	-0.142	-1.772			0.039	0.498			0.156	1.134		
SELF EST	0.034	1.064			-0.045	-1.454			0.077	1.364		
n		525				825				228		
R^2		0.1314				0.0834				0.1394		
df		511		511		811		811		214	214	

Table 3.6 *Regression Correlates of Average Lifetime Change in Economic Level continued*

Legend: AAUR = Average Annual Unemployment Rate in Area of Residence; AGE R = Age of Respondent; HGC R = Highest Grade Completed Respondent; HGC RM = Highest Grade Completed Respondent's Mother; LOCUS = Rotter Internal-External Locus of Control; SELF EST = Self-Esteem; YAFDC = Years Received Any Aid To Families With Dependent Children Benefits; YFS = Years Received Any Food Stamp Benefits; YFTWK = Years Employed as a Full-time Worker; YM = Years Married; YSSI = Years Received Any Supplemental Security Income Benefits; YUC = Years Received Any Unemployment Compensation Benefits.

Note: The regression coefficient *b* signifies how much the Average Lifetime Change in Economic Level (ALCEL) would change for every 1-unit change in each of the respective correlates. Uniqueness indices indicate the percentage of variance in the ALCEL variable accounted for by a given correlate beyond the variance accounted for by the other eleven correlates.

*** $p < .001$, ** $p < .01$, * $p < .05$

As Figure 3.6 shows, among all correlates, only HGC R, highest grade completed respondent, accounted for variance in average lifetime change in economic level (ALCEL) across sex and ethnicity/race categories, and the relationship was positive. As expected, higher levels of education were associated with greater upward mobility, while lower levels of education were associated with further downward mobility. YM, years of being married, was inversely correlated with ALCEL for black and white males and for white females. Lifetime upward mobility decreased the longer black and white men and white women were married and increased the longer they were not married. While length of marriage signified declining economic circumstances for black and white men and for white women, it had little effect on the ALCEL of black and Hispanic women and Hispanic men.

The background variable HGC RM, highest grade completed respondent's mother, was correlated with variance in ALCEL for each sex and ethnicity/race group except white men and Hispanic women. The relationship was inverse, signifying that greater levels of education of respondents' mothers, and by extension more human capital and better economic circumstances of respondents' parents in general in 1979, were associated with increasingly downward mobility. This seemingly contraindicative result for all groups, except white men and Hispanic women, suggested that respondents with better educated mothers started out in 1979 at higher economic levels (ELs) than did those whose mothers were less educated. An examination of HGC RM by economic level or decile ranking (EL) in 1979 and by sex and ethnicity/race shows that this was the case. Mothers of black males in the first EL in 1979, for example, had completed 9.8 years of education, compared to 12.5 for those in the tenth EL; mothers of white women in the second EL completed 11.1 years of education, compared to 12.7 for those in the ninth; and mothers of black women in the third EL completed 10.5 years of education compared to 11.9 for those in the eighth. As Table 3.4 illustrated, respondents whose families were in the upper ELs in 1979 had less room to move upward and were likely to have downward average lifetime economic mobility. The inverse relationship between HGC RM and ALCEL therefore reflects differences in starting economic positions for all groups except white men and Hispanic women.

The above finding also signified that the economic fortunes of white men and Hispanic women over the course of their maturing years were tied less to background than other factors. As noted, education played a role for both groups. The only other factor associated with average lifetime change in economic level (ALCEL) for Hispanic women, however, was YUC, number of years they received unemployment compensation benefits. The relationship between ALCEL and YUC was inverse, signifying that greater number of years these respondents received unemployment compensation benefits was associated with increased downward mobility.

Public benefits other than unemployment compensation associated with average lifetime change in economic level (ALCEL) were YFS, years respondents received Food Stamps, and YSSI, years they received Supplemental Security Income. YFS accounted for variance in ALCEL only for black women, while YSSI did only for white men. For black women, the relationship between YFS and ALCEL was inverse, signifying greater number of years they received these benefits was associated with increased downward mobility. For white men, the relationship between YSSI and ALCEL was positive, signifying that the greater number of years they received these benefits was associated with greater upward mobility, while fewer years of receipt were correlated with less downward mobility. Finally, YFTWK, years of full-time work, was associated with ALCEL only for black and white women. The relationship between YFTWK and ALCEL was positive, signifying that increased work effort by these women was accompanied by upward economic mobility.

In regard to the psychological correlates, neither internal-external locus of control (LOC) nor self-esteem (SELF EST) accounted for any variance in ALCEL in any sex and ethnicity/race group.

Discussion

This chapter sought to determine (1) the extent to which economic mobility among families increased or decreased, (2) the levels and trends of economic well-being among families in the lowest and highest economic levels, (3) the relationship between class and economic mobility, (4) how lifetime changes in economic levels varied by sex and ethnicity/race, (5) what human capital, demographic, and psychological characteristics correlated with lifetime economic mobility, and (6) how significant correlates of lifetime economic mobility varied by sex and ethnicity/race in regard to a youth cohort as it entered its primary working years between 1979 and 1993.

In regard to the first, the most notable finding was the increasing proportion of respondents who lived in families whose economic level remained relatively stable regardless of class. As the cohort matured, the economic fortunes of their families became increasingly locked into place, such that over time, the likelihood of respondents living in poor families escaping poverty as well as those living in affluent families experiencing downward mobility decreased. This "econosclerosis" or hardening of the economic arteries, so to speak, was disproportionately experienced by respondents living in poor families. The incidence of economic stability among respondents living in poor families increased to a greater degree than that of those living in affluent or middle class families. This "econosclerotic" trend among those living in poor families in part accounted for the seemingly more positive finding of decreased proportions of respondents who lived in families which entered poverty as a result of downward mobility. To the extent that fewer respondents lived in families which escaped poverty, the pool of respondents who lived in potentially poor families decreased. Perhaps most unsettling was the related finding that after 1986, respondents living in poor families demonstrated no upward mobility at all.

The increased incidence of economic stability between 1979 and 1993 and the lack of any upward mobility after 1986 among respondents living in poor families did not necessarily mean that they were worse off. Amidst the gray cloud of "econosclerosis" there was a silver lining, of sorts. As noted in Chapter 2 and corroborated again above, the income-to-poverty ratio of those among the lowest or first decile ranking of families (which included all poor families and some slightly above the poverty threshold) had an upward trend. Although increasing percentages of respondents lived in poor families which remained poor between 1979 and 1993, they did so at higher levels of economic well-being. This finding to some extent challenges the rationale underlying open-ended redistributionist social policies such as automatically increasing taxes of middle income and affluent families to give assistance to poor families regardless of economic trends or levels of need. It fails to satisfy basic, albeit arguable, principles of social and economic justice, such as the Pareto optimum (Gordon, 1980; Rescher, 1966) and the Difference Principle (Rawls, 1971 and 1993), which stipulate income redistribution primarily to those who are worse off in real terms than they were prior to economic growth. Although conditions meeting these principles were found for the working population and their families as a whole throughout the

1980s and early 1990s (Blank, 1997; Caputo, 1995b; Danziger and Gottschalk, 1993 and 1995), findings here indicated that such was not the case for this subset of the youth cohort as it matured into its prime family formation and working years.

In addition to the levels and trends of economic mobility and well-being among families in the lowest economic level or first decile ranking, the second question of the chapter also addressed the uppermost or tenth level. As was the case with respondents living in poor families, the incidence of those living in affluent families demonstrating no change in economic level from one year to the next increased as the cohort matured. Concomitantly, while the percentage of respondents living in non-poor families which became poor declined over time, the percentage of those living in non-affluent families which became affluent also declined. And while those in poor families demonstrated no upward mobility after 1986, those in affluent families experienced no downward mobility for all but two of the 15 years in the study period. Given the increased percentage of respondents living in affluent families likely to remain so over time, fewer respondents were likely to live in affluent families even though they may have moved into the top economic level from a lower level in the preceding year. Nonetheless, as was the case with those living in poor families, the fewer respondents who were likely to move into affluent families did so at a higher level of economic well-being after 1986. Hence, as was the case for the working population and their families as a whole, for this youth cohort, the rich got richer throughout the 1980s and early 1990s (Blank, 1997; Caputo, 1995b; Danziger and Gottschalk, 1993 and 1995; Levy and Michel, 1991).

The third issue this chapter addressed was the relationship between class and economic mobility. Because levels of economic well-being increased over time, changes in class could occur within economic levels for both poor and affluent families. This meant that respondents living in poor families could escape poverty but still find themselves in the same relative position as many of those in near-poor families. That is, given the measure of economic mobility used here, namely a change from one decile ranking to another, many respondents living in poor families which escaped poverty would still remain in the lowest or first decile ranking, thereby demonstrating no upward mobility per se. This finding in part supports Kelso (1994) who stressed the importance of focusing on economic mobility and related strategies and policies aimed at improving human capital when addressing the issue of poverty. Such policies stressing education and skill acquisition would be both morally compelling and politically viable during economic expansions when the likelihood of increasing levels of economic well-being among poor families was greatest. Nonetheless, they may be less morally compelling, though still politically troublesome in an anti-statist, anti-government climate characteristic of the 1980s and 1990s, than income maintenance measures characteristic of the more expansive welfare state decades between the 1940s and 1970s (Armey, 1995; Barbour, 1996; Bloch, 1996; Caputo, 1994; Gingrich, 1995; Katz, 1989; Weisberg, 1996).

Despite some families escaping poverty and others exiting affluence without demonstrating economic mobility due to the rise of economic well-being, the distribution of entrants and exits was remarkably uniform across class lines. That is, much economic mobility was confined to movement within one or two decile rankings from the previous year. Those respondents who lived in families that became poor, for example, were largely drawn from the ranks of those who had dropped one or two decile rankings from the previous year, while those who lived in families that became affluent were largely drawn from the ranks of those who had climbed one or two deciles.

Likewise, those who lived in families that entered the middle class had been, in roughly equal proportions, drawn from those whose families had either lost or gained one or two economic levels or decile rankings. In general, while the economy expanded and "econosclerosis" nonetheless spread, upwardly mobile respondents who lived in poor families made relatively modest gains, while those in downwardly mobile affluent families had modest losses. In addition, over time, the proportion of those living in families experiencing either extreme upward or downward mobility declined, thereby reaffirming the overall trend in decreased mobility within the cohort. These findings suggested that any initiatives to increase economic mobility more than might be possible otherwise would have a greater likelihood of success if targeted to workers in the earlier stages of family formation.

The fourth issue this chapter addressed was how lifetime changes in economic levels varied by sex and ethnicity/race. As expected, the families of white respondents in general and, to a lesser degree than was the case with income inequality and economic well-being, those of white men in particular, fared fairly well. Among respondents whose families started out in the lower decile rankings in 1979, those of white men and women had greater average upward economic mobility than did those of Hispanic males, black males, and Hispanic females, all of whom in turn had significantly greater upward mobility than families of black females. Among all families in the uppermost deciles, many had roughly the same level of downward mobility, thereby signifying a more equitable distribution of relative advantage among respondents who lived in more affluent families. In the middle decile rankings, the families of white male respondents demonstrated the most upward mobility and the least downward mobility relative to some families of other sex and ethnicity/race groups, but here again, the relative start position had more of an equalizing effect. Thus, the upward lifetime economic mobility of the families of white males was on occasion virtually indistinguishable, for example, from that of the families of Hispanic males and white females, but was greater than that of black males and Hispanic females.

Also as expected, in light of findings in regard to income inequality and economic well-being in Chapters 1 and 2, was the plight of the families of black women. On the whole, regardless of start position, the families of black females demonstrated the least upward mobility and the most downward mobility relative to other groups. Of all the findings, this one is perhaps the most troublesome. This is so, in part, because, as Jones (1985 and 1998) has so richly described, black women have historically felt the weight of racial discrimination compounded by sexual prejudice. Despite reports of partially successful compensatory efforts since the 1970s to remedy the effects of discrimination and to promote job mobility among women in general (Blank, 1995), the findings of this study suggest, ceteris paribus, that relative to other sex and ethnicity/race groups, young black women even in the best of times can look forward to less upward and greater downward economic mobility as they enter their prime working and family formation years.

Factors associated with economic mobility were the subjects of the last two issues raised in this chapter. Of the dozen factors examined and controlled for, only one, education level, was found to be correlated with economic mobility for all sex and ethnicity/race groups. In general, higher levels of education were associated with greater upward mobility, while lower levels of education were associated with further downward mobility.

Education is a human capital variable, one that can be readily targeted to increase the economic opportunities of potentially disadvantaged groups, such as young black women in particular, while concomitantly appealing to the broader public in general. As such, its importance cannot be stressed too much. Any policy initiatives seeking to maximize the prospect for upward mobility and minimize the extent of downward mobility should have an educational component that targets youth in general and black female youth in particular. Several such initiatives will be a subject of the next chapter.

Black women also benefited from full-time work, as did white women. The longer these women worked in full-time jobs, the greater the economic mobility of their families. This finding presents a dilemma reflected in the welfare reform legislation passed by Congress in 1996. The Personal Responsibility and Work Opportunity Reconciliation Act obliges participating states to get increasing percentages of their welfare rolls into jobs, with little or no attention paid to type, whether full-time or part-time. On the one hand, economically disadvantaged women are being strongly encouraged, if not forced by the prospect of time-limited benefits, to work, but as Blank (1997) has amply demonstrated and others (e.g., Murnane and Levy, 1996) forcefully argue, the labor market conditions at present and as anticipated offer few prospects of full-time, let alone well paying, jobs for such women. On the other hand, the 1996 Act's stress on jobs virtually precludes further formal education. Given that young economically disadvantaged women, particularly such black women, with lengthier full-time employment work histories and with higher levels of education demonstrated greater levels of upward mobility, the 1996 Act appears to be at cross-purposes with its goal of self-sufficiency in any meaningful sense. Once off the welfare rolls, these women are not likely to demonstrate much upward mobility, but rather remain, as Edin and Lein (1997) have shown, in a struggle to make ends meet.

Much has been said about the relation between the economic well-being and marriage among black Americans. In the 1960s, then Assistant Secretary of Labor Daniel Patrick Moynihan (U.S. Dept. of Labor, 1965) inadvertently launched two decades of relative silence with a report on the demise of the black family and the economic plight of increasing proportions of black women raising children by themselves. Contemporary scholars (e.g., McLanahan and Sandefur, 1994; Wilson, 1987) have redressed this silence and reopened the debate, in part noting the increased economic well-being among "intact" or two-parent black families and thereby reaffirming, as some (e.g., Duncan, 1984) had found among the poverty population in general, that marriage is a mode of economic advancement. For many, when viewed as a cross-sectional event, marriage results in an immediate increase or decrease in economic level, thereby respectively signifying upward or downward mobility. But the longer term consequences, economically speaking, are ambiguous.

In this 15-year study, length of marriage accounted for no variance in economic mobility beyond that of other factors among black women, nor among Hispanic men or women. For these maturing groups of youth, the immediate impact of marriage or its dissolution had no lasting or net effect on their average lifetime economic mobility. Furthermore, years of being married was found to be inversely correlated with net changes in economic mobility for black and white males and for white females. For these maturing groups of youth, lifetime upward mobility decreased the longer they were married and increased the longer they were not married. Hence, for many maturing youth, marriage as a route for upward economic mobility may be a hard sell. On the one hand, the immediate benefit for those for whom marriage serves as an escape from poverty might nonetheless lock them into a near-poverty existence. On the other hand, postponing or

◆ Advantage White and male, Disadvantage Black and Female forgoing the immediate economic benefit of marriage until a more propitious time might increase the prospect for greater upward economic mobility in the longer run.

Findings related to economic mobility shed additional light on popular and scholarly literature reporting on the erosion of the American Dream, that is, that the present generation may have lower standards of living than their parents (e.g., Levy and Michel, 1991; Newman, 1993; Rubin, 1994; Zill and Nord, 1994). Given that the cohort only entered its primary working and family formation years between 1979 and 1993, the inverse relation found between economic mobility and level of education of respondents' mothers for most sex and ethnicity/race groups was expected. In 1979, most respondents lived in their parents' households, and were likely to have been at high points of economic well-being. As they formed their own families and households, members of the youth cohort, particularly those starting out at higher levels of economic well-being in 1979, were expected to lose some economic ground in their early working years, with the prospect of realizing the American Dream still before them. Unexpected, however, was the finding that the inverse relation between economic mobility and level of education of respondents' mothers did not hold, to a statistically significant degree, for white males and Hispanic females. In their early family formation and prime working years, the economic mobility of white men and Hispanic women was less tied to their parents' economic fortunes. They had neither gained nor lost economic ground on average relative to their circumstances in 1979, and as such would have little or no catching up to do while pursuing higher standards of living than their parents in future years.

The role of public benefits in economic mobility was ambiguous, in part reflecting differences in the programs. No relationship between net economic mobility and length of time on Aid to Families with Dependent Children was found. This finding was consistent with the previous finding regarding increased percentages of respondents living in families getting locked into a particular class level, whether poor, middle, or affluent. Over time, increasing percentages of respondents living in poor families, some of whom were AFDC recipients, remained poor. To attribute the lack of economic mobility to receipt of AFDC, as do two of the most vociferous proponents of welfare reform throughout the 1980s and 1990s, namely Mead (1996) and Murray (1996), would be too much of a stretch of this finding.

The climate of opinion throughout the 1980s and early 1990s regarding "dependency" and "self-sufficiency" was such that any reliance on government assistance was viewed with increasing suspicion and decreasing legitimacy. Findings of this study about other assistance programs suggested that such wholesale condemnation might be misguided. The correlation of net economic mobility and of public assistance programs other than AFDC varied by sex and ethnicity/race groups. For two of the programs, Unemployment Compensation and Food Stamps, the relation to net economic mobility was as expected, namely inverse. The longer length of time families of Hispanic women received Unemployment Compensation benefits and families of black women received Food Stamps, the more downward economic mobility they experienced. These findings reflected the higher levels of family income beneficiaries of these programs.

Unemployment Compensation has no means test attached to it and Food Stamps eligibility can reach 130% of the poverty threshold. Hence, unlike many AFDC families that were by definition poor and thereby had nowhere lower to move, Unemployment Compensation and Food Stamp beneficiaries had room beneath them, and their economic levels fell the longer they were users. The downward mobility of families with black females that received Food Stamp benefits corroborated other study findings regarding the economic plight of this sex and ethnicity/race group. Continued use of Food Stamps and net downward economic mobility reflected the larger picture of limited economic well-being of the families of black women in general. Hispanic women, on the other hand, lived in more affluent families than did black women. The net declines in economic mobility of these families that received Unemployment Compensation benefits in part reflected the relatively low level of the benefit compared to the former wage.

The findings in regard to families of white males and receipt of Supplemental Security Insurance benefits, though unexpected, reaffirms the advantage of these families compared to other sex and ethnicity/race groups. SSI is a federally financed and administered program that targets economically needy individuals determined to have justifiable reasons for non-labor-force participation (e.g., being aged or having a disability). Its monthly payments are about one-and-a-half to two times higher than those of AFDC families and as such may be sufficient to lift those whose family income hovers just below the lowest of the ten tiers of economic well-being into the second tier. Given the greater level of economic well-being of families of white males in general, they would be the ones most likely in any given year to have incomes at the high end of many, if not all, economic levels, including the lowest tier. Hence, for low-income families of white males, SSI serves as a vector for upward economic mobility.

Finally, neither of the psychological variables, internal-external locus of control nor self-esteem, accounted for any variance in net economic mobility in any sex and ethnicity/race group. These findings reaffirmed those of Duncan (1984) who found little influence of psychological and attitudinal attributes on income dynamics, but failed to corroborate those of Caputo (1999), Dolinsky, Caputo, and O'Kane

(1989), and Goodwin (1983) who, on varying measures of economic well-being and psychological attributes, found otherwise. Although internal-external locus of control was found in Chapter 2 to be correlated with economic well-being among black women and self-esteem, for white men and women, findings of this chapter in part corroborate Kelso (1994), who suggested that efforts to enhance economic mobility, and by extension, reduce poverty, had a better chance of successful impact to the extent that they focused on skill acquisition and educational achievement rather than on motivational, attitudinal, or psychological attributes per se. Toward these ends, Chapter 4 summarizes and integrates the major findings of this study in regard to income inequality, economic well-being, and economic mobility among the youth cohort and, in light of the findings, discusses a range of policy options meant to reduce poverty rates, increase the level of economic well-being, and the like.

Chapter 4
SUMMARY AND IMPLICATIONS

Introduction

This study examined income inequality, economic well-being, and economic mobility among families in a youth cohort between 1979 and 1993. Results suggested a murkier portrait than the oft-repeated aphorism that the rich got richer and the poor got poorer with the economic expansion of the 1980s. On one hand, the "econosclerotic" nature of economic mobility meant that increasing percentages of respondents living in poor or affluent families respectively remained poor or affluent between 1979 and 1993. On the other hand, both affluent and poor families in the youth cohort were better off economically when using measures such as median family income adjusted for inflation and the income-to-poverty ratio. Such findings for the youth cohort, though at variance with related studies of the general population (e.g., Blank, 1997), in part challenge the rationale underlying open-ended redistributionist social policies, such as automatically increasing taxes of middle income and affluent families to give assistance to poor families regardless of economic trends or levels of need. At issue in prosperous times is to what level of material existence Americans are willing to allow economically disadvantaged families to rise, in an absolute sense, despite the inevitable controversies associated with measures of poverty (Ruggles, 1990), before their sense of justice and fairness regarding redistribution of income is eclipsed by their related concerns as overburdened taxpayers and financially strapped consumers.

To the extent the quality of life among economically disadvantaged families rises as the economy does, basic, albeit arguable, principles of social and economic justice, such as the Pareto optimum (Gordon, 1980; Rescher, 1966) and the Difference Principle (Rawls, 1971 and 1993) are not satisfied, while the populist proposition that prosperity should be shared is met (Reich, 1997). These principles justify government intervention for purposes of income redistribution on the grounds that it benefits primarily those who are worse off in real terms than they were in less economically robust times. Although conditions meeting these principles were found for the working population and their families as a whole throughout the 1980s and early 1990s (Blank, 1997; Caputo, 1995b; Danziger and Gottschalk, 1993 and 1995), the upward trend in economic well-being among poor families found for this youth cohort and the stagnant or downward trend found for the general population raise conundrums for changes in social policy targeting low-income families.

To the extent the economic circumstances of America's youth improve at an acceptable level and rate as they form their own families and negotiate the labor market in their prime working years, further income redistribution becomes morally and politically less viable for this segment of the population. Yet, for those older, more mature labor market participants still in their prime working years, that is, those between 34 and 54 years of age, whose economic well-being might stagnate or worsen during an expanding economy, further redistribution becomes morally and politically more justifiable. In addition, to the extent some families are increasingly likely to become locked into poverty as young parents mature, then redistributionist policies can be justified to ensure a level of economic well-being in an absolute sense below which no family should be allowed to fall.

Broad-based appeals for redistributionist policies taking more from affluent taxpayers and targeting the "stagnant" middle class, a mantra of the Clinton administration and "progressive" political pundits (e.g. see Greenberg, 1995; Greenberg and Skocpol, 1997b), may find political favor, but they may also extend benefits, and hence, costs, more than if a targeted approach could be found that bypassed younger, maturing workers whose economic well-being is likely to rise without such efforts. To the extent, however, that the level of economic well-being of youth forming their own families and entering their prime working years remains unacceptably low in an absolute sense, even if rising, then such broad-based appeals are that much more compelling morally and politically.

An expanding economic pie throughout the 1980s and early 1990s did not mean, as Blank (1997) and others (e.g., Caputo, 1995b; Danziger and Gottschalk, 1993 and 1995; Karoly, 1993) have convincingly demonstrated for the working population as a whole, that portions or slices were evenly distributed throughout the cohort of youth by class, sex or ethnicity/race. Median income of both poor and affluent families increased for all groups within the youth cohort examined in this study, but levels varied by class, sex or ethnicity/race. The families of white respondents in general and those of white males in particular started in more economically advantaged positions than did families of black and Hispanic youth and they sustained higher levels of economic well-being as the cohort matured into its prime family formation and working years.

Affluent families experienced more equitable income by sex and ethnicity/race and generally steeper increases in median income. They were more uniformly better off, having strongly positive gains in total income between 1979 and 1993. With the exceptions of 1987 and 1992, affluent families demonstrated virtually no income disparity regardless of sex and ethnicity/race. Poor families, on the other hand, differentially experienced increased income, with men in general and black men in particular having more modest rising increases in family income between 1979 and 1993 than women. On the whole, poor families exhibited varying degrees of income disparity, reflecting the differential increases in total income throughout the study period. Income disparity between affluent and poor families increased for those of black males and decreased for those of white women.

Among all sex and ethnicity/race groups examined in this study, the plight of black women in general and those who lived in poor families in particular stands out and calls for interventions aimed at improving their economic well-being. The strongest case for income redistribution and for affirmative action can be made for maturing black women living in poor families. The findings of this study suggest that universal policies targeting all mothers, or all women, all parents, all workers, and the like, though politically appealing to broader constituencies, would nonetheless enhance the prospects for increased economic well-being and upward economic mobility among maturing black women living in poor families the least and the related gains made would be modest at best.

Results of the study indicated that maturing black women benefit from full-time work, as do white women. Black women who live in poor families can benefit most from full-time jobs. To the extent labor market conditions are or remain such that these women can command only low-wage, part-time, or contingent jobs, then measures such as the Personal Responsibility and Work Opportunity Reconciliation Act of 1996 might have the unintended adverse consequence of miring them in poverty or near-poverty conditions. Given the adverse consequences of poverty to (1) the children of black women who live in poor families, in terms of their physical and mental well-being and life chances, (2) society's loss of their potential productivity and income, (3) additional incurred medical costs associated with low-weight births and hospital emergency care, and (4) the increased poverty these women are likely to experience in old age due to low-wage work histories (Caputo, 1997c; Disney, 1996; Duncan and Brooks-Gunn, 1997; Edin and Lein, 1997; Ozawa, 1995), more intensive and adequately funded efforts are necessary to increase the likelihood that maturing black women living in poor families obtain sufficient resources and skills requisite to balancing full-time employment and family responsibilities at an acceptable level of economic well-being.

Study findings cast doubt on the rhetoric equating receipt of public assistance with decreased economic mobility. For the study sample as a whole, the number of years families received Aid to Families with Dependent Children benefits explained no variance in economic mobility beyond that of other factors, thereby casting further doubt on the wisdom of the Personal Responsibility and Work Opportunity Reconciliation Act of 1996, which ended the Federal entitlement of and set time limits on cash assistance (CQ 1996 Almanac, 1997a). These provisions of the 1996 legislation were justified in large part by the rationale that cash assistance caused dependency or decreased upward mobility of poor families. Such was not the case for any of the sex and ethnicity/race groups in this study, not even for black women, many of whom, as single parents disproportionately receiving welfare, bore the brunt of such claims.

As noted in Chapter 3, for black women in the study, only receipt of Food Stamps was associated with economic mobility. The correlation was inverse, that is, greater use was associated with less mobility. Although the 1996 legislation tightened eligibility requirements for

Food Stamps and added work requirements and time limits for able-bodied recipients between the ages of 18 and 50 who do not have dependents, historically much of the rhetoric against public assistance that fueled the welfare reform debates in the 1980s and 1990s was directed primarily at AFDC, not the more broadly supported Food Stamps program (Burton, 1992; Katz, 1996; Katz, 1989; Kelso, 1994; Mead, 1996; Murray, 1996). Hence, reduced welfare rolls and decreased reliance on cash public assistance, currently known as Temporary Assistance for Needy Families (TANF), which replaced AFDC and has a cap on Federal expenditures, are associated with the goal of self-sufficiency inherent in the 1996 legislation. Food Stamps remain available for anyone deemed eligible, thereby enabling the program to expand and contract with demand, and its use is not scrutinized either to the extent AFDC was nor TANF is (Katz, 1997).

A Defense of Affirmative Action

At issue in regard to public provision is, in part, the extent to which policies and programs meant to benefit black women and their families in general and respective poor families in particular should be guided by class, gender, and race-conscious principles. Much of the contemporary concern about affirmative action centers around race-conscious principles. President Clinton's call for a "national conversation on race" and his appointment of a commission headed by historian John Hope Franklin to report on the current state of race relations in part reflect sustained, vigorous debate throughout the 1980s and 1990s on the merits of affirmative action programs seeking greater social and economic integration primarily along racial lines (Clinton, 1997a and b; D'Souza, 1995; Hacker, 1992; Murray, 1984; Steinberg, 1995; Thernstrom and Thernstrom, 1997). Often these debates are cast in dichotomous terms: Should efforts to help disadvantaged individuals, families, or groups focus on race or on class? When such concerns conflict, which should prevail? In regard to affirmative action programs in particular, which policies are more deserving-class-based approaches that help both white and black ethnicity/race groups or race-based approaches that help both affluent and poor black Americans? The explicit addition of sex further compounds these already contentious questions.

Recent strategies to roll back the legislative victories of the civil rights movement, such as California's Proposition 209 and the Civil Rights Act of 1997 proposed by Senator Mitch McConnell (R-KY) and Representative Charles Canady (R-FL), call for the elimination of affirmative action for women and people of color in public-sector hiring, contracting, and education. Such initiatives, if respectively upheld and passed, would weaken legal protection against sex discrimination, from the tougher requirement that such instances withstand judicial "strict scrutiny" to a much looser one permitting any sex discrimination deemed "reasonably necessary" to the smooth functioning of society (Reed, 1997). Reviewing the literature on the effects of affirmative action, Hartmann (1996) concluded that enforcement of the Federal Contract Compliance Program and Title VII of the Civil Rights Act had modest effects in the intended direction. That is, these provisions helped women and people of color somewhat, after adjusting for all other effects. On the whole, none of the research Hartmann reviewed supported the notion that affirmative action in employment helps the best educated most. The observed progress for women and people of color resulted in large part from increased educational opportunities. Affirmative action invariably helps higher educated women and people of color, just as it benefits other workers who are discriminated against. Nonetheless, Hartmann found no evidence that affirmative action helps them more than others.

Given the importance of education and work to the economic well-being and mobility of black women and their families, affirmative action programs aimed at improving their skills and full-time labor force participation can be quite beneficial. As indicated in Chapter 2, the wages of black women contributed about half as much to total family income as did that of white males in 1993. Hence, maturing black women can increase their economic well-being with greater opportunities for full-time, higher paying employment. At issue in part is the question of access. Examining a cohort of mature women in the 1980s and 1990s, for example, Caputo and Cianni (1997) found that employed black women lacked access to on-the-job training (OJT) programs and they disproportionately participated in clerical training programs, while white women were disproportionately represented in administration and management training programs. Caputo and Cianni also found that OJT completion rates were comparable between black and white women and that over time OJT contributed to higher wages regardless of race. In regard to OJT access, however, the advantage nonetheless remains with white men (Pouncy and Mincy, 1995). Lynch (1989) has shown that among the employed, young white workers are twice as likely to train within a firm either through an apprenticeship or other forms of OJT. Hence, affirmative action on the part of employers to ensure that their maturing black female employees gain access to OJT programs in general and in administrative and management programs in particular are steps in the right direction, although, as noted below, other targeted measures can be taken within the context of more universal programs.

Opponents of affirmative action, however, have noted that race-preferential policies in effect have redistributed black workers from small and medium-size firms to large companies and federal jobs and that such policies rest on the premise that the destiny of the black community lies in what others do, or fail to do (e.g., Woodson, 1996). To offset a culture of victimization and to capitalize on the capacity of the U.S. economy to create jobs in the small-business sector, Woodson (1987) extols the virtue of entrepreneurs and encourages black Americans to set up their own businesses. Given the study's finding in regard to locus of control, namely that maturing black women with strong beliefs in self-determination have greater levels of economic well-being than those more likely to attribute what happens to them to fate or luck, affirmative action targeting equality of opportunity and access can be defended. In a related national longitudinal study of mature women, Dolinsky, Caputo, and Pasumarty (1994) found that between 1969 and 1989 black women were far less likely to become entrepreneurs than white women, but once they did so, they were only marginally less likely to stay. As with training, at issue were barriers to requisite resources regarding access. Affirmative action programs designed to ensure access to entrepreneurial opportunities or to OJT can increase the likelihood of more economically rewarding work experiences for maturing black women. Two relatively recent Supreme Court decisions upheld the principles of affirmative action. In the 1989 case *Richmond v. J.A. Croson Co.* the Court invalidated a set-aside program for African-American businesses but nonetheless permitted, albeit more narrowly tailored, race-conscious relief. In the 1995 case *Adarand Constructors, Inc. v. Pena*, the Court reaffirmed the Croson standards, albeit also more narrowly tailored. Hence, the principle of sex-conscious relief, by extension, still stands in principle (Berry, 1996).

Given the *Croson* and *Adarand* decisions, the presidential call to mend rather than end affirmative action makes sense (Clinton, 1995b). While addressing the National Archives and Records Administration, Clinton urged all Federal agencies to apply four standards of fairness to affirmative action programs: no quotas in theory or practice; no illegal discrimination of any kind; no preference for people who are not qualified for any job or other opportunity; and as soon as a program has succeeded, it must be retired. The first three standards have been implemented and debated with varying degrees of rigor, but with an overriding, albeit uneasy consensus about their merits and meaning since 1969 when the Nixon administration announced the Philadelphia Plan which amounted to mandatory quotas for the hiring of minority group members on Federal construction projects (Caputo, 1994). Given reliance on the dubious nature of statistical disparities as evidence of ongoing discrimination, affirmative action programs lacked any viable criteria to signal when a program should end. Neither in the address to the National Archives and Records Administration nor in the memorandum to the heads of executive departments and agencies did Clinton offer criteria or guidelines of what might constitute sufficient evidence of success to justify ending a specific program (Clinton, 1995a).

Study findings here, however, suggest a way to signal, if not an end, at least a shift in focus, to specific affirmative action efforts successfully targeted toward young black women. The income-to-poverty ratio can be used as a yardstick to measure success of affirmative action efforts aimed at the families of black women. Ideally, the goal should be to ensure that wage-related income of such families be a substantial portion, say above 75-80%, of total family income and that total family income equal or exceed their respective poverty thresholds within and for a specified period of time, thereby ending poverty as they know it. To the extent this is too ambitious or unrealistic in a practical or economic sense, then a more modest goal would be to ensure that wage-related income of such families be above 60-65% of total family income and that total family income reach at least 75-80%

of the poverty line. When the goal is met and sustained for a designated period of time, say one complete business cycle, then affirmative action efforts for this targeted group can cease. Other sex and ethnicity/race groups can be likewise targeted to the extent wage-related income and the income-to-poverty ratio of their poorest members fall below either the modest or ambitious goal. To the extent the full-time wage-related income criterion is met and the income-to-poverty ratio criterion falls short despite full participation in affirmative action efforts, then government ought to make up the difference. This can be achieved, among other ways, through the Earned Income Tax Credit (EITC) program which already enjoys bipartisan support and currently raises incomes for many of the working poor by as much as 40%, at a taxpayer cost of about 0.4% of the gross domestic product (Krugman, 1997).

Given some findings of this study, proposals designed to strengthen the family as an institution in general, such as making divorce more difficult or encouraging marriage between unwed teenage mothers and the fathers of their children as occurred in earlier generations (Coontz, 1997; Popenoe, 1990), may appear to circumvent class-race-sex dilemmas but in effect they might somewhat justifiably reduce the sex and ethnicity/race gap in economic well-being by adversely affecting white men. As noted previously, this study found that with the exception of white males, families with married respondents had higher levels of economic well-being in any given year than those with widowed, separated, or divorced respondents. This finding supported the growing literature on economic and other disadvantages associated in general with single-parent families, the vast majority of which are female-headed, whether due to widowhood, separation, or divorce regardless of race (McLanahan and Sandefur, 1994; Mead, 1996). Universal appeals encouraging marriage therefore might in effect close the sex and ethnicity gap in economic well-being to the extent greater proportions of both white men and black women were married. If this were to occur, the economic well-being of maturing young white men would stay steady or fall and that of maturing young black women would rise. To the extent lengthier marriages were found to be associated with decreased economic mobility, over time the intact families of black women and those of white men would be locked into increasingly caste-like classes. For black women this would mean higher levels of economic well-being in an absolute sense than otherwise possible, albeit at lower relative levels of economic status (that is, slightly above or below poverty thresholds) for a significant proportion of them. For white men this would mean lower levels of economic well-being in an absolute sense, albeit at higher relative levels of economic status for many of them.

Findings from this study also suggest that sex plays a larger role than race in regard to the economic well-being of families, but that nonetheless both still matter. To the extent universal or sex- and gender-neutral policies are likely to benefit white males and females to a greater degree than their Hispanic and black counterparts, selective or targeted responses are more appropriate. However, the merits of targeted programs must be balanced against society's willingness to finance far more adequately and to meet a greater variety of needs than in times past programs designed for poor families, particularly those disproportionately comprised of single mothers and, even more so, of black single mothers. Given the relative economic advantage among respondents living in white families in general and among white male respondents in particular found in this study, additional resources needed to fund such programs can be justifiably obtained by taxing more affluent families and corporations and redistributing that income to meet a variety of family and labor-market related needs of black women in general and black women living in poor families in particular. To achieve such ends, a combination of universal-like and targeted programs is in order. As noted above, the goal of such efforts should be to end poverty as these families know it, namely to raise their wage-related income to a specified percentage of total family income and to raise total family income above either 75-80% or 100% of the poverty thresholds. Given related study findings, strategies geared toward economic mobility per se become instrumental to these ends and assume lesser importance once these two other goals are met.

What follows are several principles and related proposals meant to increase the prospects of economic well-being and economic mobility that, in theory, could benefit anyone taking advantage of them, but which can also be targeted to areas having higher concentrations of black women living in poor families. In establishing such programs, the study's finding that young black women who held strong beliefs about control of one's life through self-determination had higher levels of economic well-being than those who believed more strongly in fate, luck, or chance should be kept in mind. This finding suggests that efforts to enhance opportunity for these women could be furthered by strengthening the sense of self-efficacy in those already demonstrating strong beliefs in self-determination and by nurturing it in those more likely to attribute what happens to them to fate, luck, or chance. Though no correlation was found with economic mobility, belief in self-determination was associated with higher levels of economic well-being among black women regardless of class. Hence, principles and programs that respectively stress and impart skills aimed at increasing economic mobility and that also seek to promote self-determination at the very least increase the likelihood that less mobile adherents and participants might nonetheless enjoy a higher level of economic well-being than they might have otherwise.

Principles and Strategies Designed to Increase Human Capital

Appropriate principles and policies can be derived from the experiences of school-to-work initiatives that sprouted in the early 1990s in response to changes in the economy and the reported mismatch between skills employers claimed they needed in young workers and the lack of preparedness of these young workers (Olson, 1997). Reports of ten such National Youth Apprenticeship Initiatives monitored by Boston-based Jobs for the Future indicated some work-related segmentation along racial lines. Pouncy and Mincy (1995) reported that most white youth participating in these initiatives between 1992 and 1994 were in manufacturing, business, and technical fields, whereas most minority youth were in health technician and teaching assistant slots, or in jobs linked to employers who cannot easily leave urban labor markets. Regarding gender composition, young women increasingly entered fields such as electronics and metalworking in which they were previously not well represented.

Following on the heels of the National Youth Apprenticeship Initiative and bipartisan support during the 1992 presidential campaign, in 1994 Congress overwhelmingly passed the School-to-Work Opportunities Act (STWOA) with national business and education support (CQ 1994 Almanac, 1995). The National Association of Manufacturers, the National Alliance of Business, the U.S. Chamber of Commerce, the Committee for Economic Development, the National Coalition for Advanced Manufacturing, and the National Employer Leadership Council all supported the law. The act provided limited seed money, $695 million through fiscal 1996, to states to help carry out school-to-work plans. By the fall of 1996, these initiatives, encompassing hundreds of programs across 37 states, linked educational institutions and businesses in such a way as to combine academic and work-site instruction for high school students (Olson, 1997). In so doing, they lay the foundation for lifelong learning necessitated by increasingly global market forces and technological changes. STWOA embodies five elements for successful programs: academic instruction, vocational skills training integrated with academic or remedial instruction, work-based education coordinated with school-based instruction, connection of every program to the next in a hierarchy of education and training opportunities, and applied teaching methods and team-teaching strategies (Grubb, 1996). Of these elements, the most crucial are linking programs in vertical ladders and integrating instruction and support services.

Based on academic and work-site research, Murnane and Levy (1996) identify three sets of basic skills and five principles necessary to do well in work environments increasingly subjected to exponential rates of change due to global markets and innovative technologies. They base these skills and principles on their observation that "widening earnings gap between high school and college graduates stems in large part from differences in the mastery of basic skills *when the two groups were high school seniors*" (p. 8, italics in original). More highly educated individuals get the better-paying jobs in large part because employers have surmised that college graduates are far more likely to have stronger basic skills than those high school graduates who failed to go to college. Basic skills needed for a continually changing work environment that pays well, however, can readily be taught in high school. By examining employee-recruiting and work practices in firms paying high wages, Murnane and Levy identified the growing importance of these three sets of skills:

The "hard" skills: basic mathematics, problem-solving and reading abilities at levels much higher than many high school graduates now attain.

The "soft" skills: the ability to work in groups and to make effective oral and written presentations- skills many schools do not teach

The ability to use personal computers to carry out simple tasks such as word processing (p. 9)

Firms that succeeded in continually improving their product embrace five common principles:

Ensure that all frontline workers understand the problem.

Design jobs so that all frontline workers have both incentives and opportunities to contribute to solutions.

Provide all frontline workers with the training needed to pursue solutions effectively.

Measure progress on a regular basis.

Persevere and learn from mistakes; there are no magic bullets (p. 14).

Although anyone can benefit from acquisition of these basic skills during high school and application of these principles in the workplace, findings from this study of a youth cohort suggest that a universal approach would still leave young black women at a disadvantage relative to other sex and ethnicity/race groups. Hence, a conscientious effort targeted to high schools that have high concentrations of black females and to employers who can hire them would greatly increase the likelihood of their moving out of poverty-level low-wage jobs into higher-wage middle class jobs. Toward this end, state officials can pool the state-of-the-art knowledge regarding learning and accordingly apply modified basic academic strategies appropriate for employment-related environments. They can build on successful school-to-work efforts, as well as those state-financed training programs, many of which were created in the late 1980s in response to a growing perception that the private sector was providing less than the optimal amount of training (Bassi, 1995). Though these latter programs varied considerably across the 46 states having at least one such program in 1990, evaluation research findings were consistent with the idea that education and/or training was most valuable when it occurred within firms (Moore and Blake, 1992; Moore, Wilms, and Bolus, 1988). Though the specifics of such an approach outlined here are beyond the scope of this chapter, the principles behind a unified education and training system build upon institutions and programs already in place. Olson (1997) and Grubb (1996) lay out what needs to be done on the part of business, government, and academic institutions to make successful school-to-work opportunities an increasing reality for youth and young adults. Given findings from previous studies regarding high drop-out rates in those programs requiring high exit skills, however, successful, large-scale skills programs for urban youth will require earlier interventions that increase academic skills before these youth enroll in school-to-work programs (Pouncy and Mincy, 1995). Such effort will invariably require a greater financial commitment than currently allotted.

School-to-work programs, per se, do little for those who drop out of school and, hence, cannot be reached by such efforts. Earlier efforts in the 1980s to reach this population through the Job Training Partnership Act indicated no gains from participation (Blank, 1994). Out-of-school youth present formidable obstacles to any effort directed at increasing their work effort or their work-related income. For these youths, Pouncy and Mincy (1995) propose a targeted demand-side strategy aimed at reducing bias in employer-financed training. Many employer-financed training proposals enable employers to spend a certain fraction of their payroll costs to train their own low-skilled workers, or they may contribute to a public training program (Baily, Burtless, and Litan, 1993). Given increased costs associated with private OJT for low-skilled workers and investment loss incurred when trained workers depart for other firms, many firms are reluctant to make the expenditures required to train their own low-skilled workers. However, if all employers were to make such investments (or pay a training tax), any single firm's incentive to poach another's trainees would be removed. To offset the white male advantage associated with the present pattern of OJT participants and to encourage firms to incur necessary costs associated with training low-skilled workers, Pouncy and Mincy offer three alternatives. One scheme is to use the public fund created by firms who prefer to pay the "training tax" to supplement current public expenditures for "disadvantaged" employment and training programs. These programs, such as those sponsored by the Job Training Partnership Act, currently serve disproportionate numbers of people of color. Such a scheme, however, would only exacerbate the current two-tier training system in which young white workers receive employer-provided training and other young workers receive government training.

A second solution for reducing bias in employer-financed training would be to exempt or reduce training expenditures and taxes if firms employed larger fractions of previously unemployed young workers. Although these workers are more likely to be people of color, this solution would in all likelihood steer such workers to firms that provided no training. A third solution, preferred by Pouncy and Mincy (1995), would be to use the public training fund to subsidize training in firms that hired more previously unemployed workers, allowing the subsidy to increase as a function of the post-training wage. Thus, firms might compete for training grants based on their ability to increase the post-training wages of previously unemployed or underemployed, low-skilled workers. The result would be to increase training investment in young workers of color in general, while special efforts can be made to ensure equal access for young black women. Encouraging firms to hire and train previously unemployed young workers is consistent with research suggesting that employers respond best to non-stigmatizing interventions (Burtless, 1985; Palmer and Barth, 1978) (e.g., a new jobs tax credit) and worst to highly targeted interventions (e.g., training tax subsidies for welfare recipients). Given findings of the present study, employers agreeing to hire and train previously unemployed youth should nonetheless take steps to ensure equal access for young black women, some of whom may or may not be welfare recipients, but many of whom might otherwise be destined for lifetimes of low-wage work (Edin and Lein, 1997).

To maximize school-to-work transitions, Lerman (1996) proposes a universal youth apprenticeship system. Modeled on the approach practiced in Germany, Denmark, Switzerland, and Australia, such a system would embody a contractual arrangement between employers, workers, and schools, whereby a seventeen- to eighteen-year-old combines work-based and school-based learning over a two- to three-year period to achieve a certified competency in a career field along with a high school degree. Although this model entails a universal to ensure given standards of academic and skill-based competencies, its main benefits would flow to non-college workers, particularly for minority youth. As envisioned, the apprenticeships would (1) equalize access to jobs by providing a formal mechanism in which employers can have confidence and can try out at-risk workers, (2) expose young people to constructive adult peer groups, and (3) allow employers to watch young people as they learn critical skills. In addition, an early job-related start is critical to improve incentives and to avoid serious trouble. To the extent that adult job responsibilities are postponed, many at-risk youth are likely to become involved in crime or unwed parenthood.

Developing an infrastructure sufficient to support a youth

apprenticeship system would take time. Nonetheless, Wisconsin, New York, Pennsylvania, and Maine already operate viable youth apprenticeship programs and, as noted, the School-to-Work Opportunities Act (SWOTA) provides seed money to help states undertake similar activities and build broad-based systems. Finally, after several years of debate, Congress reached agreement on revamping the myriad of job-training programs, in effect repealing the Job Training and Partnership Act passed during the Reagan administration. The Workforce Investment Partnership Act of 1998 consolidated about sixty federal job-training programs into three block grants to the states, and it expanded a program of eight hundred model, one-stop career centers that combine training, employment services, unemployment insurance, vocational rehabilitation, adult education, and other programs in one "street-level" location. To the extent that high schools and community colleges can successfully link with these centers in their efforts to enhance school-to-work transitions, prospects for improving a more solid foundation for a youth apprenticeship system are thereby increased (CQ 1997 Almanac, 1998; H.R. 1385, 1998).

Although low basic skills contribute to low employment levels and wages, they do not by themselves preclude access to unsubsidized jobs (Maynard,1995). For example, nearly 90% of young males with lower-than-average reading skills are employed, compared to only half of similarly skilled females. In contrast, the employment rate differential between lower-skilled and higher-skilled young single female parents is only 6 percentage points- 49% versus 55% (Strain and Kisker, 1989). Even among welfare recipients, while there is a strong correlation between their measured skills and labor-market success, a sizable portion of those who gain employment have low measured skills (Burghardt and Gordon, 1990; Maynard, Nichelson, and Rangarajan, 1992; Rangarajan, Kiskar, and Maynard, 1992). Percentages of welfare recipients not meeting minimum skill requirements have been reported to vary from 61 for sales workers, 55 for clerical/secretarial, 40 for service occupations, 37 for crafts and construction, 33 for household workers, and 31 for manual operatives (Zill, Moore, and Stief, 1991). Although skills count in regard to obtaining employment, Maxfield (1988) has reported that employers invariably identify social skills and work habits as being as important, if not more so, than basic reading and math skills for low-end jobs. Employers may need to be encouraged to rethink their job structure to accommodate lower-skilled individuals enroute to higher-skilled, higher paying jobs (Berryman, 1988). Supported work demonstration projects in the mid-1980s, for example, resulted in more than 70% of long-term welfare recipients holding unsubsidized jobs through transitional support, job redefinition, and natural time trends (Hollister, Kemper, and Maynard, 1984).

Strategies to Improve Labor Market Conditions

Strategies to improve labor market conditions include efforts to improve the rewards for low-wage work, while expanding the economy as a whole. As noted above, one of the more effective strategies for rewarding low-wage work and, by extension, arguably (Phelps, 1997), expanding the pool of full-time low-wage workers, is the Earned Income Tax Credit (EITC). In 1993, EITC was expanded as part of the Omnibus Budget Reconciliation Act (CQ 1993Almanac, 1994), and by the end of the decade it was projected to cost about $25 billion, making it the largest cash or near-cash program directed toward low-income families with children (Committee on Ways and Means, 1996; Haveman, 1995; Howard, 1997). Although Mead (1996) contends that the EITC is not a viable strategy to reduce poverty because it is not likely to increase work hours, Blank (1994) attributes the relatively small effect of this refundable tax credit on labor supply to lack of information about the program. Some eligible workers may not know about it and hence not receive it. The program is run through the tax system and is unrelated to other job training and income transfer programs, which are run out of local welfare and employment offices. Hence, government officials whom most poor people are in contact with, namely caseworkers, are not well informed about the EITC. Other eligible individuals may be discouraged from using it since they will not find out how much they will receive until they have filed their tax returns. In addition, the EITC has a somewhat complex structure with rising and falling subsidy rates depending on level of income, making subsidies difficult to understand. Efforts to increase the take-up rate of the EITC may increase labor force participation among those Mead claims have little motivation to work.

To improve the earning capacity of families with maturing black females in general and black single-headed families in particular, the EITC can be expanded to cover all parents who have any school-age or younger children living at home and whose full-time wage-related portion of total family income and total family income fall below designated levels of the income-to-poverty ratio. For example, the EITC can be implemented to ensure that full-time wage-related income with the credit comprise at least 75-80% of total family income (or 60-65% in a less ambitious scheme) and that total family income (also with the credit) equal or exceed the poverty thresholds (or 75-80% of it in a less ambitious scheme) within and sustained for a specified period of time (e.g., a complete business cycle). If the more ambitious scheme were put into place, poverty as we know it would end. Currently, most beneficiaries receive a large enough supplement to ensure that full-time work, together with Food Stamps, raises them out of poverty. In the more ambitious scheme proposed here, EITC would raise full-time low-wage families above poverty without benefit of Food Stamps. Since the eligibility for Food Stamps, based on gross income, is 130% of the poverty threshold, many low-wage families could still receive benefits.

Given that the EITC is financed through taxes, the cost of ending poverty can also be shared with the private sector by raising the minimum wage. Blank (1994) notes that the EITC is particularly effective in reducing poverty when interacted with the minimum wage. On August 20, 1996, President Clinton signed into law legislation increasing the minimum wage for an estimated 10 million workers from $4.25 to $4.75 an hour on October 1, and then to $5.15 an hour on September 1, 1997 (CQ 1996 Almanac, 1997b). Approval of the legislation marked the end of one of the most bitter and largely partisan battles of the 104th Congress, with Republican leadership against and many Democrats and some Republicans from the Northeast and Midwest in support. The measure passed both chambers of Congress by fairly wide margins, 354-72 in the House and 76-22 in the Senate. Congress last approved a minimum wage increase in 1989, effective in 1990 and 1991, and the purchasing power stood at a 40-year low. Opponents argued that an increase in the minimum wage would cause job loss, but many economists claimed the loss would be small in contrast to the number of workers who would continue to hold a job and earn higher wages (Rubin, 1996; Rubin and Weisman, 1996).

Synthesizing five years of published studies on the minimum wage, Card and Krueger (1995) reported, among other things, that contrary to the predictions of textbook models, increases in wages were accompanied by increases in employment. In addition, increases in the Federal minimum wage in 1990 and 1991 were estimated to led to significant increases in wages for workers at the bottom of the wage distribution, and to a reduction in overall wage disparity. About one-third of workers whose wages were affected by the 1990 and 1991 increases in the Federal minimum wage lived in families in the bottom 10% of the earnings distribution. Increases in the minimum wage led to increases in the lower percentiles of family earnings and to an increase in the share of earnings going to families at the bottom of the distribution. The magnitude of the earnings transferred by the 1990-1991 increases in the Federal minimum wage was relatively small-about 0.2% of total earnings, or $5.5 billion per year. Hence, to the extent that increases in the minimum wage are modest, the same can be expected in regard to their actual effects on the standard of living of families with low earnings. To the extent that increases in the minimum wage are greater than the modest levels of the 1990s, however, and by extension resulting in higher standards of living for low-wage workers and their families, then the public can expect to pay higher prices in such establishments as fast-food restaurants to absorb the increase.

On the whole, the 1996 increase in the minimum wage was rather insubstantial. In real terms, the increase to $5.15/hr. recouped only about half the ground lost over the previous years and it affected only a fraction of the service-sector workforce. The next sensible step is another increase in the minimum wage to $7.50/hr. at least, thereby restoring the full real value of the minimum in 1968, which was $6.50 in inflation-adjusted values (Galbraith, 1998). Such an adjustment in the minimum wage will enable more working poor families to escape poverty than has been found for the $5.15/hr. rate (Houseman, 1998).

Another strategy to improve the prospect of accepting low-wage work is a reemployment bonus, that is, a payment made to an unemployed individual when he or she accepts a job offer (Bassi, 1995). This strategy can be particularly useful and relatively cost-effective in high unemployment areas where it can be targeted to encourage more rapid reemployment of economically disadvantaged sex and ethnicity/race groups, thereby lowering the overall unemployment rate in the area. A reemployment bonus can be designed to make the payment for which an unemployed individual is eligible a declining function of the length of time that an individual is unemployed. The idea behind this design is that by increasing the implicit cost of postponing acceptance of a job, the unemployed person has an incentive both to search for work more intensely and to accept jobs that he or she might otherwise refuse. Alternatively, the payment could be a fixed amount.

Experimental studies on the effects of reemployment bonuses among recipients of Unemployment Insurance indicated that the bonuses operate primarily by increasing the intensity of individuals' job search efforts, rather than by inducing the unemployed to accept lower-paying jobs (McMurrer, 1993). Simulations by Davidson and Woodbury (1993), however, indicated that displacement resulting from reemployment bonuses can be substantial, thereby reducing the overall increase in employment that results from bonuses. To the extent that use of reemployment bonuses targeted toward young black women might be likely to displace black men, results of the present study suggest that other strategies should be tried, given that the economic well-being of the families of black males, though improved between 1979 and 1993, were nonetheless at levels below all other sex and ethnicity/race groups except those of black women. This is not to suggest that displacement of individuals from other groups should be ignored, only that their ability to bounce back might be greater. Since displacement adversely affects anyone to whom it occurs, reemployment bonuses should be used with caution.

There are those who argue that globalization of the economy has created conditions making work less remunerative than in years past for the vast majority of labor force participants. Wolman and Colamosca (1997), for example, have shown that, as measured in 1994 dollars, the median earnings of "management-related occupations" fell from $34,389 in 1987 to $32,608 in 1994, although when measured in mean income, the picture improves from $40,313 in 1987 to $41,887 in 1994. The higher mean incomes reflect the huge increase in the salaries paid to the captains of capital, that is, those who derive more of their income from assets such as stocks, bonds, trusts, business equity, and non-home equity. Stagnated hourly wages contributed to declines in real family income growth despite increases in annual hours worked throughout the 1980s and 1990s.

To the extent businesses and capital can take advantage of lower-wage labor, regardless of skill levels, wherever they can find it, those employed in the higher-paying Western world are likely to see further losses in the remuneration of their work effort than those employed elsewhere. Worse yet, to the extent technological change in a global economy produces wider gaps between greater productive capacity and falling consumer purchasing power, work itself may end as we currently understand it. There may not be an actual reduction of jobs and a literal loss of work, as Rifkin (1995) maintains, but the full-time, full-year job with benefits such as health insurance and viable pensions may become anachronisms for many (Tilly, 1996). Those who extol the virtues of the market yet denounce government interventions as a retardation of economic growth may find themselves in paradoxical positions of supporting such policies as paying supplemental benefits to those who work less than whatever becomes the normal working hours, a practice common among European countries, or extending subsidies targeting low-wage full-time work primarily for mothers, a practice with bipartisan support in the United States, to full-time low-wage parents at least, and perhaps even to all full-time workers. To the extent part-time or contingency work becomes the norm, then subsidies may be expanded for these workers also.

For our purposes, Phelps (1997) offers a novel but nonetheless plausible solution to the problem of low-wage work. He proposes a graduated schedule of government subsidies to each qualified enterprise (that is, private sector employer or company) for every full-time low-wage worker in its employ. All such employees having the same wage would bring in the same subsidy to the employer. Likewise, government contributes the same additional subsidy with every additional employee costing the employer a given hourly wage. The subsidy would take the form of tax credits against the company's tax liability, that is, its payroll and corporate income tax (Chase, 1997).

Essentially, as wage cost per hour increases, the subsidy per hour decreases. For example, at the low end of the wage scale eligible for subsidies, a wage of $4.00 per hour would result in a subsidy of $3.00 per hour for a gross wage per hour of $7.00; while at the high end of the wage scale eligible for subsidies, a wage of $12.00 per hour would result in a subsidy of $0.06 per hour for a gross wage per hour of $12.06. The calibration is such that the subsidies decline at a rate to discourage employers from lowering the level of low-wage or near low-wage hourly work to take advantage of the benefits. In addition, the schedule can be calibrated or adjusted periodically so that the wage of workers with the lowest productivity, namely those with the lowest wage cost per hour, can be pulled up half the distance to the prevailing median wage, while wage rates closer to that mark are pulled up by a smaller fraction of the gap. Given that the country is not about to revert to a family wage and hence use family size to determine an appropriate benchmark, bringing the lowest productive paid workers up to half the median will nonetheless go a long way toward reducing the gap between family income and official poverty thresholds.

Phelps (1997) justifies the government outlay on the grounds that it equals the external or social benefit representing the employed worker's contribution to society. These contributions to society emerge from the employed worker's ability to support oneself and to exercise responsibility as a citizen, community member, parent, and the like. Society at the least recoups the subsidy, if not more, due to the offsetting reduction in the costs of welfare, medical care, unwanted pregnancies and births, crime, and other maladies. It should be noted that society would likewise recoup the costs of implementing any of the measures proposed here to the extent they increase the likelihood of full-time employment of low-wage workers in general.

Although Phelps (1997) may place too much faith in the disciplinary aspects of work to affect the behavior of young low-wage workers, his plan simultaneously addresses labor force participation rates and wage levels. Many plans focus on one or the other. For example, the 1996 welfare reform legislation, the Personal Responsibility and Work Opportunity Reconciliation Act, which ended the Federal mandate for cash assistance and placed time limits on benefits, may reduce the welfare rolls, may or may not increase labor force participation, and is silent on the matter of wage levels (CQ 1996 Almanac, 1997a). The 1996 act assumes that work has inherent rewards benefiting the individual and society regardless of wage level. Phelps also believes in intrinsic personal and social value of work, but at levels sufficient to sustain a livable standard. Also, the earned income tax credit (EITC), as Phelps notes, is not really a tool to reward and stimulate the employment of low-wage workers, so much as a program of credits for those who, for whatever reason, have low-wage incomes-

and not over a lifetime but in a current year. Additionally, in some scenarios due to the complex structure of the EITC, some beneficiaries may find themselves working less up to a point where doing so begins to cost a loss of the credit.

Phelps's employer subsidy plan, however, always results in low-wage workers getting higher levels of pay that at the least approximate a livable standard, thereby encouraging greater labor force participation among those disinterested in the former or lower wage and greater incentives or even higher wages for all low-wage workers. Although Phelps (1997) proposed his plan for hourly wages on a national basis for all full-time low-wage workers, nothing precludes state experimentation with more targeted sex and ethnicity/race groups, like young black women, or for all low-wage workers while applying affirmative action principles to ensure participation by young black women.

Conclusion

In conclusion, the proposals presented here are based on the assumption that work has become the operative norm for all able-bodied adults, even mothers of young children, that will guide social policy. The overwhelming bipartisan support for passage and implementation of the Personal Responsibility and Work Opportunity Reconciliation Act is indicative of this operative norm. Women are in the work force to stay, not because of policies such as the 1996 welfare reform legislation, but rather due in part to changing labor market conditions that have rewarded their work with rising wages relative to men's losses and to social forces promoting greater expectations that sex equity, a desideratum in and of itself, can only be achieved by greater labor force participation (Blank, 1994; Coontz, 1997). Prior to passage of welfare reform legislation in 1996, many of the debates about government's responses to poverty focused on the merits of proposals and programs designed to balance the need for income maintenance and requirements for work. In the end, those who advocated for paternalistic enforcement of requirements aimed to increase work effort (e.g., Mead, 1996) won. To abandon discussion of income maintenance at an acceptable level of economic well-being in light of this "victory," however, would be a mistake. Paternalistic efforts that focus on self-sufficiency may reduce dependency of low-income families on government largesse, but still leave many bereft of resources necessary for a quality of life conducive to being responsible and responsive parents and raising healthy and productive children. As Johnson (1996) has reminded us, poverty remains the social problem that needs to be addressed and related issues go beyond the scope of individual work effort.

Government, in bipartisan fashion, must direct resources to those programs determined to be successful with those who are poor, who in turn should have an opportunity to participate in the design of programs for their benefit. In addition, society at all levels must embrace personal responsibility and a commitment to sex and ethnicity/race equity. It is unfortunate that Congress refused to incorporate funds for formal efforts to evaluate the effects of the 1996 welfare reform legislation. Failure to do so only increases the likelihood that political rhetoric will determine what constitutes success or failure, with little if no systematic attention given to either who benefits or how so by the legislation. Quality-of-life issues entail more than the social expectation that self-sufficiency is a sufficient goal of individual effort, particularly if it results in persistent poverty for themselves and their families. We will need constant reminders that economic well-being encompasses more than the creation of an environment predicated primarily on job-related opportunities and self-sufficiency, as important as these may be.

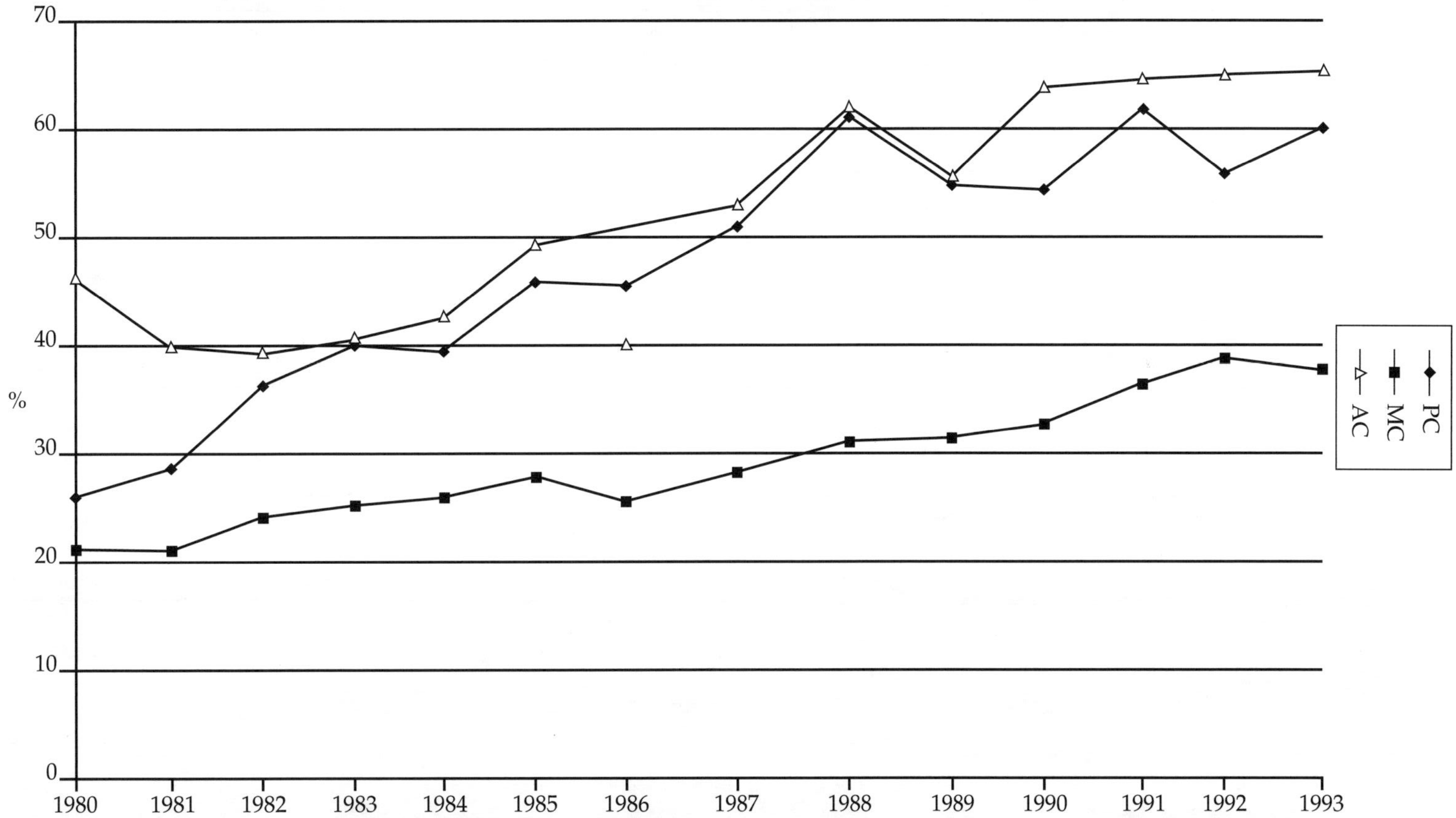

Figure 3.1 Trends in the Percentage Distribution of Respondents Who Demonstrated No Change in the Income-to-Poverty Ratio (IPR) Percentile Ranking, 1980-1993 Legend: AC = Affluent Class, MC = Middle Class, PC = Poor Class

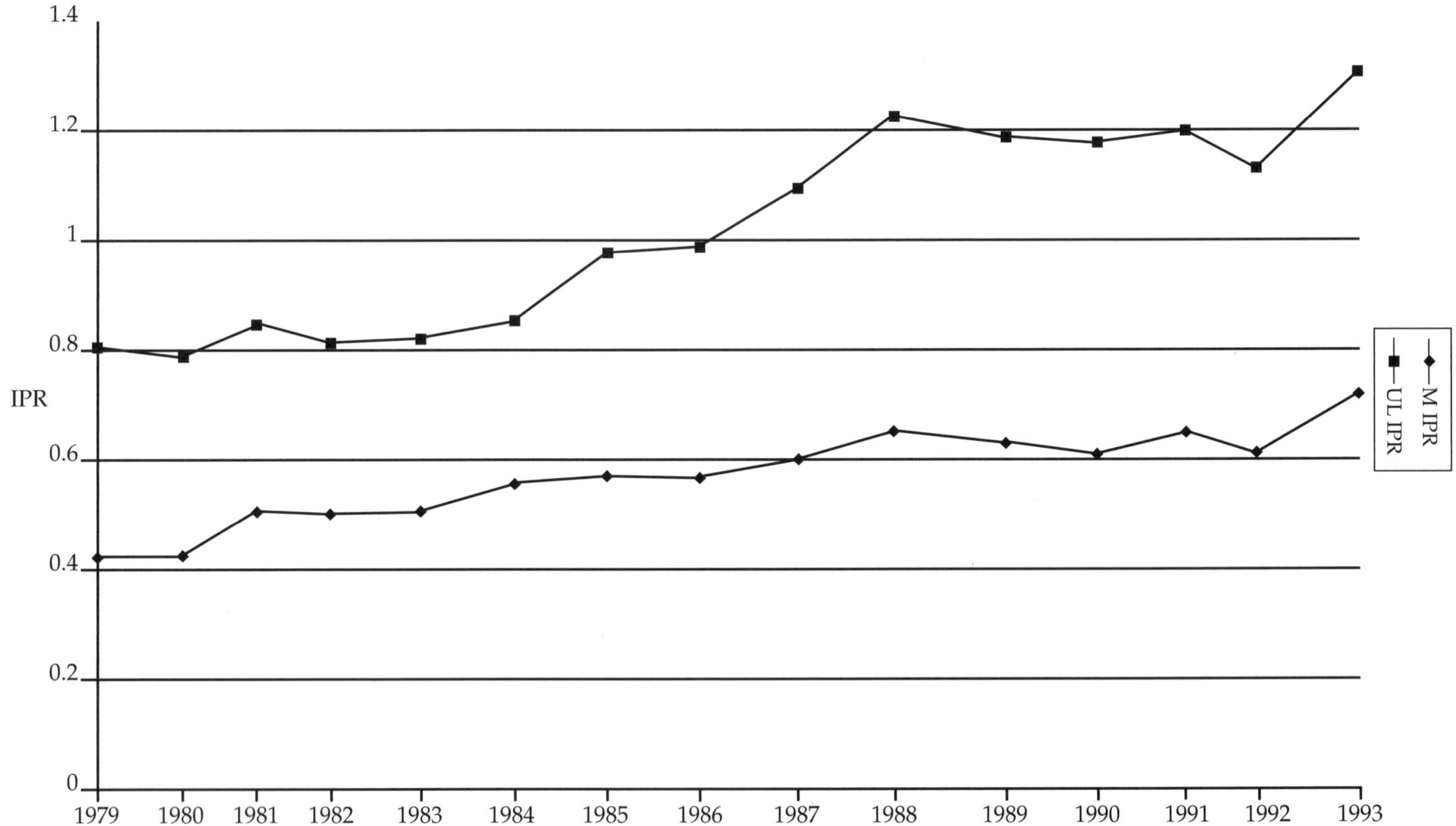

Figure 3.2 Trends of the Income-to-Poverty Ratio (IPR) Mean and Upper Limit for the Lowest Economic Level, by Year

Legend: M IPR = Mean Income-to-Poverty Ratio; UL IPR = Upper Limit of Income-to-Poverty Level

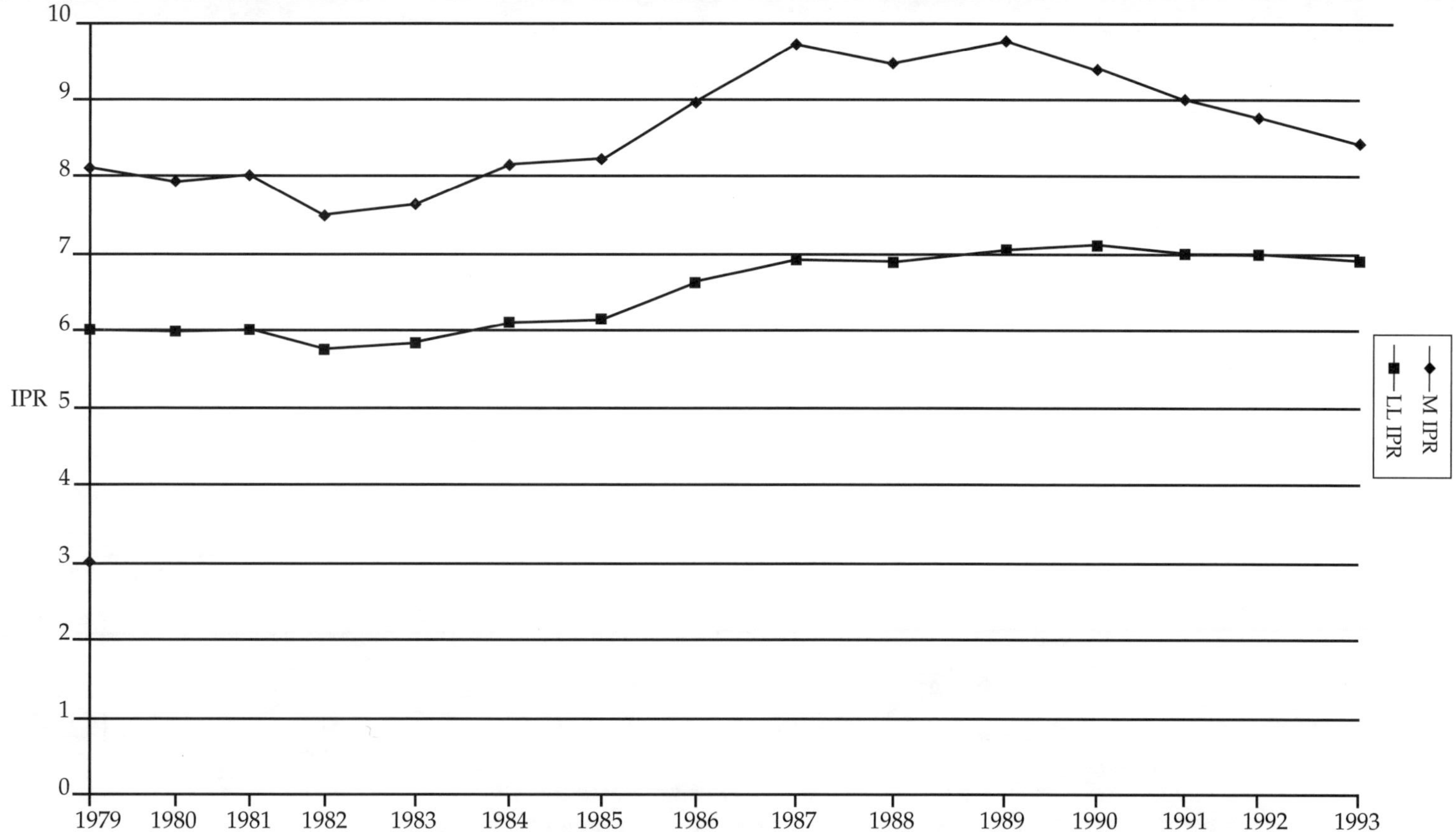

Figure 3.3 Trends of the Income-to-Poverty Ratio (PR) Mean and Lower Limit for the Top Economic Level, by Year

Legend: M IPR = Mean Income-to-Poverty Ratio; LL IPR = Lower Limit of Income-to-Poverty Level

APPENDIX

Table A.1 *Correlates of Economic Well-Being (Income-to-Poverty Ratio), 1980 1, Entire Study Sample (N=2745)*

	Beta Weights[2]		Uniqueness Indices[3]		
CORRELATES:			Uniqueness		
Background Variables:	Beta	t[4]	Index	F[5]	*b*[6]
Age of Respondent		-0.652			-0.017
Highest Grade Completed, R	0.090	4.224[a]	0.005	17.86[a]	0.114
Highest Grade Completed, RM	0.195	10.148[a]	0.032	102.98[a]	0.130
Hours Worked/Year (10^{-2})	0.249	12.339[a]	0.047	152.30[a]	0.608
Marital Status (1=married)		1.705			0.165
Residence (1=within SMSA)		-0.206			-0.007
Unemployment Rate	-0.039	-2.207[c]	0.001	4.87[c]	-0.010
Change Variables:					
Change in Family Size	-0.103	-5.896[a]	0.011	34.76[a]	-0.126
Change in Hours Worked	-0.106	-5.388[a]	0.009	29.03[a]	-0.339
Psychological Variables:					
Locus of Control		-1.652			-0.400
Self-Esteem	0.065	3.425[a]	0.004	11.72[a]	0.033
INTERCEPT					-0.684
R Square	0.1623				
Adjusted R Square	0.1589				
F	48.123[a]				

[1] Since this part of the study incorporates changes in family size and hours worked from one year to the next as correlates, the first year of reported results in 1980 reflects changes from 1979. [2] Beta weights are standardized multiple regression coefficients obtained when the Income-to-Poverty Ratio was regressed on all eleven predictors. [3] Uniqueness indices indicate the percentage of variance in the Income-to-Poverty Ratio accounted for by a given predictor variable beyond the variance accounted for by the other ten predictors. [4] For *t* tests that test the significance of the beta weights df = 2744. [5] For F tests that tested the significance of the uniqueness indices df = 1, 2744. [6] *b* is the regression coefficient, signifying by how much the IPR will change for every 1-unit change in the correlate-variable. Beta Weights and Uniqueness Indices appear only for those variables that met statistical significance.

[a] $p < .001$; [b] $p < .01$; [c] $p < .05$.

Table A.2 *Correlates of Economic Well-Being (Income-to-Poverty Ratio), 1987, Entire Study Sample (N=2745)*

	Beta Weights[1]		Uniqueness Indices[2]		
CORRELATES:			Uniqueness		
Background Variables:	Beta	t[3]	Index	F[4]	*b*[5]
Age of Respondent		0.000			0.000
Highest Grade Completed, R	0.220	11.661[a]	0.035	136.02[a]	0.241
Highest Grade Completed, RM	0.105	5.930 a	0.009	35.18[a]	0.083
Hours Worked/Year (10^{-2})	0.287	16.202[a]	0.069	262.58[a]	0.773
Marital Status (1=married)	0.129	7.745[a]	0.015	60.00[a]	0.646
Residence (1=within SMSA)	0.084	4.793[a]	0.006	22.98[a]	0.519
Unemployment Rate	-0.052	-2.946[b]	0.002	8.68[b]	-0.144
Change Variables:					
Change in Family Size	-0.976	-5.917[a]	0.009	35.02[a]	-0.203
Change in Hours Worked	-0.084	-4.918[a]	0.006	24.19[a]	-0.359
Psychological Variables:					
Locus of Control	-0.040	-2.451[c]	0.001	6.00[c]	-0.065
Self-Esteem	0.084	4.540[a]	0.005	20.61[a]	0.048
INTERCEPT		-3.492[a]			-3.136
R Square	.2815				
Adjusted R Square	.2786				
F	97.349[a]				

[1] Beta weights are standardized multiple regression coefficients obtained when the Income-to-Poverty Ratio was regressed on all eleven predictors. [2] Uniqueness indices indicate the percentage of

variance in the Income-to-Poverty Ratio accounted for by a given predictor variable beyond the variance accounted for by the other ten predictors. [3] For *t* tests that test the significance of the beta weights df = 2744. [4] For F tests that tested the significance of the uniqueness indices df = 1, 2744. [5] *b* is the regression coefficient, signifying by how much the IPR will change for every 1-unit change in the correlate-variable. Beta Weights and Uniqueness Indices appear only for those variables that met statistical significance.

[a] $p < .001$; [b] $p < .01$; [c] $p < .05$.

Table A.3 *Correlates of Economic Well-Being (Income-to-Poverty Ratio), 1993, Entire Study Sample (N=2745)*

	Beta Weights[1]	Uniqueness Indices[2]			
CORRELATES:			Uniqueness		
Background Variables:	Beta	t[3]	Index	F[4]	*b*[5]
Age of Respondent		0.504			0.011
Highest Grade Completed, R	0.281	15.019[a]	0.067	225.60[a]	0.256
Highest Grade Completed, RM	0.083	4.687[a]	0.006	21.86[a]	0.057
Hours Worked/Year (10^{-2})	0.285	16.082[a]	0.068	258.67[a]	0.682
Marital Status (1=married)	0.088	5.323[a]	0.007	28.34[a]	0.389
Residence (1=within SMSA)	0.111	6.669[a]	0.012	44.26[a]	0.619
Unemployment Rate		0.844			0.035
Change Variables:					
Change in Family Size	-0.038	-2.384[c]	0.001	5.68[c]	-0.104
Change in Hours Worked	-0.044	-2.579[b]	0.002	6.65[b]	-0.171
Psychological Variables:					
Locus of Control	-0.035	-2.175[c]	0.001	4.51[c]	-0.050
Self-Esteem	0.054	3.072[b]	0.002	9.44[b]	0.028
INTERCEPT		-3.599[a]			-3.186
R Square	0.2863				
Adjusted R Square	0.2834				
F	99.664[a]				

[1] Beta weights are standardized multiple regression coefficients obtained when the Income-to-Poverty Ratio was regressed on all eleven predictors. [2] Uniqueness indices indicate the percentage of

variance in the Income-to-Poverty Ratio accounted for by a given predictor variable beyond the variance accounted for by the other ten predictors. [3] For *t* tests that test the significance of the beta weights df = 2744. [4] For F tests that tested the significance of the uniqueness indices df = 1, 2744. [5] *b* is the regression coefficient, signifying by how much the IPR will change for every 1-unit change in the correlate-variable. Beta Weights and Uniqueness Indices appear only for those variables that met statistical significance.

[a] $p < .001$; [b] $p < .01$; [c] $p < .05$.

Table A.4 *Correlates of Economic Well-Being (Income-to-Poverty Ratio), 1980 [1], Black Males (N=326)*

	Beta Weights [2]		Uniqueness Indices [3]		
CORRELATES:			Uniqueness		
Background Variables:	Beta	t[4]	Index	F[5]	*b*[6]
Age of Respondent		-0.711			-0.040
Highest Grade Completed, R		1.967			0.115
Highest Grade Completed, RM	0.228	4.308[a]	0.046	18.56[a]	0.124
Hours Worked/Year (10^{-2})	0.230	3.654[a]	0.033	13.35[a]	0.398
Marital Status (1=married)		-0.913			-0.292
Residence (1=within SMSA)		-0.232			-0.014
Unemployment Rate		-1.323			-0.135
Change Variables:					
Change in Family Size	-0.189	-3.728[a]	0.035	13.90[a]	-0.147
Change in Hours Worked		-1.959			-0.231
Psychological Variables:					
Locus of Control		-1.769			-0.092
Self-Esteem	0.111	2.025[c]	0.010	4.10[c]	0.038
INTERCEPT		-0.084			-0.121
R Square	0.2185				
Adjusted R Square	0.1911				
F	7.982				

[1] Since this part of the study incorporates changes in family size and hours worked from one year to the next as correlates, the first year of

reported results in 1980 reflects changes from 1979. [2] Beta weights are standardized multiple regression coefficients obtained when the Income-to-Poverty Ratio was regressed on all eleven predictors. [3] Uniqueness indices indicate the percentage of variance in the Income-to-Poverty Ratio accounted for by a given predictor variable beyond the variance accounted for by the other ten predictors. [4] For *t* tests that test the significance of the beta weights df = 325. [5] For F tests that tested the significance of the uniqueness indices df = 1, 325. [6] *b* is the regression coefficient, signifying by how much the IPR will change for every 1-unit change in the correlate-variable. Beta Weights and Uniqueness Indices appear only for those variables that met statistical significance.

[a] $p < .001$; [b] $p < .01$; [c] $p < .05$.

Table A.5 *Correlates of Economic Well-Being (Income-to-Poverty Ratio), 1980 [1], White Males (N=663)*

	Beta Weights [2]		Uniqueness Indices [3]		
CORRELATES:			Uniqueness		
Background Variables:	Beta	t [4]	Index	F [5]	*b* [6]
Age of Respondent		0.678			0.047
Highest Grade Completed, R		0.269			0.020
Highest Grade Completed, RM	0.117	2.912 [b]	0.012	8.48 [b]	0.121
Hours Worked/Year (10^{-2})	0.174	3.785 [a]	0.020	14.33 [a]	0.457
Marital Status (1=married)		-1.773			-0.478
Residence (1=within SMSA)	0.088	2.207 [c]	0.007	4.87 [c]	0.206
Unemployment Rate		-0.641			-0.066
Change Variables:					
Change in Family Size		-0.983			-0.057
Change in Hours Worked		-1.411			-0.170
Psychological Variables:					
Locus of Control		0.351			0.019
Self-Esteem		1.297			0.029
INTERCEPT		-0.586			-0.947
R Square	0.0622				
Adjusted R Square	0.0464				
F	3.928 [a]				

[1] Since this part of the study incorporates changes in family size and hours worked from one year to the next as correlates, the first year of reported results in 1980 reflects changes from 1979. [2] Beta weights are

standardized multiple regression coefficients obtained when the Income-to-Poverty Ratio was regressed on all eleven predictors. [3] Uniqueness indices indicate the percentage of variance in the Income-to-Poverty Ratio accounted for by a given predictor variable beyond the variance accounted for by the other ten predictors. [4] For *t* tests that test the significance of the beta weights $\underline{df} = 662$. [5] For F tests that tested the significance of the uniqueness indices $\underline{df} = 1, 662$. [6] *b* is the regression coefficient, signifying by how much the IPR will change for every 1-unit change in the correlate-variable. Beta Weights and Uniqueness Indices appear only for those variables that met statistical significance.

[a] $p < .001$; [b] $p < .01$; [c] $p < .05$.

Table A.6 *Correlates of Economic Well-Being (Income-to-Poverty Ratio), 1980* [1]*, Hispanic Males (N=178)*

	Beta Weights [2]		Uniqueness Indices [3]		
CORRELATES:			Uniqueness		
Background Variables:	Beta	t [4]	Index	F [5]	*b* [6]
Age of Respondent	0.156	2.031 [c]	0.018	4.13 [c]	0.198
Highest Grade Completed, R		0.671			0.051
Highest Grade Completed, RM	0.216	2.837 [b]	0.035	8.06 [b]	0.967
Hours Worked/Year (10^{-2})		1.124			0.207
Marital Status (1=married)		-1.074			-0.433
Residence (1=within SMSA)		-0.219			-0.028
Unemployment Rate	-0.155	-2.167 [c]	0.020	4.70 [c]	-0.370
Change Variables:					
Change in Family Size	-0.337	-4.899 [a]	.106	24.03 [a]	-0.391
Change in Hours Worked		-0.472			-0.109
Psychological Variables:					
Locus of Control		-1.513			-0.130
Self-Esteem		0.903			0.031
INTERCEPT		-0.470			-1.072
R Square	0.2661				
Adjusted R Square	0.2175				
F	5.472 [a]				

[1] Since this part of the study incorporates changes in family size and hours worked from one year to the next as correlates, the first year of

reported results in 1980 reflects changes from 1979. [2] Beta weights are standardized multiple regression coefficients obtained when the Income-to-Poverty Ratio was regressed on all eleven predictors. [3] Uniqueness indices indicate the percentage of variance in the Income-to-Poverty Ratio accounted for by a given predictor variable beyond the variance accounted for by the other ten predictors. [4] For *t* tests that test the significance of the beta weights $df = 177$. [5] For F tests that tested the significance of the uniqueness indices $df = 1, 177$. [6] *b* is the regression coefficient, signifying by how much the IPR will change for every 1-unit change in the correlate-variable. Beta Weights and Uniqueness Indices appear only for those variables that met statistical significance.

$^a p < .001$; $^b p < .01$; $^c p < .05$.

Table A.7 *Correlates of Economic Well-Being (Income-to-Poverty Ratio), 1980* [1]*, Black Females (N=525)*

	Beta Weights[2]		Uniqueness Indices[3]		
CORRELATES:			Uniqueness		
Background Variables:	Beta	t[4]	Index	F[5]	*b*[6]
Age of Respondent		-0.350			-0.016
Highest Grade Completed, R		1.131			0.059
Highest Grade Completed, RM	0.159	3.640[a]	0.021	13.24[a]	0.097
Hours Worked/Year (10^{-2})	0.271	5.526[a]	0.049	28.68[a]	0.552
Marital Status (1=married)		0.839			0.171
Residence (1=within SMSA)		-0.303			-0.017
Unemployment Rate		-1.705			-0.148
Change Variables:					
Change in Family Size	-0.122	-3.010[b]	0.015	9.06[b]	-0.102
Change in Hours Worked		-2.628[b]	0.011	6.91[b]	-0.325
Psychological Variables:					
Locus of Control		-0.557			-0.023
Self-Esteem	0.088	2.039[c]	0.007	4.15[c]	0.034
INTERCEPT		-0.382			-0.473
R Square	0.1683				
Adjusted R Square	0.1505				
F	9.440[a]				

[1]Since this part of the study incorporates changes family size and hours

worked from one year to the next as correlates, the first year of reported results in 1980 reflects changes from 1979. [2] Beta weights are standardized multiple regression coefficients obtained when the Income-to-Poverty Ratio was regressed on all eleven predictors. [3] Uniqueness indices indicate the percentage of variance in the Income-to-Poverty Ratio accounted for by a given predictor variable beyond the variance accounted for by the other ten predictors. [4] For *t* tests that test the significance of the beta weights df = 524. [5] For F tests that tested the significance of the uniqueness indices df = 1, 524. [6] *b* is the regression coefficient, signifying by how much the IPR will change for every 1-unit change in the correlate-variable. Beta Weights and Uniqueness Indices appear only for those variables that met statistical significance.

[a] $p < .001$; [b] $p < .01$; [c] $p < .05$.

Table A.8 *Correlates of Economic Well-Being (Income-to-Poverty Ratio), 1980 [1], White Females (N=825)*

	Beta Weights [2]		Uniqueness Indices [3]		
CORRELATES:			Uniqueness		
Background Variables:	Beta	t [4]	Index	F [5]	*b* [6]
Age of Respondent		0.054			0.003
Highest Grade Completed, R	0.144	3.375 [a]	0.012	11.39 [a]	0.205
Highest Grade Completed, RM	0.176	4.816 [a]	0.025	23.19 [a]	0.158
Hours Worked/Year (10^{-2})	0.182	4.699 [a]	0.023	22.08 [a]	0.506
Marital Status (1=married)		0.777			0.134
Residence (1=within SMSA)		0.972			0.073
Unemployment Rate		-0.906			-0.082
Change Variables:					
Change in Family Size	-0.084	-2.546 [c]	0.007	6.48 [c]	-0.112
Change in Hours Worked	-0.121	-3.199 [b]	0.011	10.24 [b]	-0.411
Psychological Variables:					
Locus of Control		-0.390			-0.018
Self-Esteem		1.075			0.020
INTERCEPT		-1.518			-2.092
R Square	0.1322				
Adjusted R Square	0.1204				
F	11.256 [a]				

[1] Since this part of the study incorporates changes in family size and hours worked from one year to the next as correlates, the first year of reported results in 1980 reflects changes from 1979. [2] Beta weights are

standardized multiple regression coefficients obtained when the Income-to-Poverty Ratio was regressed on all eleven predictors. [3] Uniqueness indices indicate the percentage of variance in the Income-to-Poverty Ratio accounted for by a given predictor variable beyond the variance accounted for by the other ten predictors. [4] For *t* tests that test the significance of the beta weights df = 824. [5] For F tests that tested the significance of the uniqueness indices df = 1, 824. [6] *b* is the regression coefficient, signifying by how much the IPR will change for every 1-unit change in the correlate-variable. Beta Weights and Uniqueness Indices appear only for those variables that met statistical significance.

[a] $p < .001$; [b] $p < .01$; [c] $p < .05$.

Table A.9 *Correlates of Economic Well-Being (Income-to-Poverty Ratio), 1980* [1]*, Hispanic Females (N=228)*

	Beta Weights[2]		Uniqueness Indices[3]		
CORRELATES:			Uniqueness		
Background Variables:	Beta	t[4]	Index	F[5]	*b*[6]
Age of Respondent		-0.157			-0.010
Highest Grade Completed, R		0.0570			0.027
Highest Grade Completed, RM	0.177	2.927[b]	0.027	8.57[b]	0.078
Hours Worked/Year (10^{-2})	0.210	3.024[b]	0.029	9.14[b]	0.437
Marital Status (1=married)		1.283			0.282
Residence (1=within SMSA)		0.080			0.007
Unemployment Rate		-1.771			-0.236
Change Variables:					
Change in Family Size	-0.234	-3.909[a]	0.048	15.28[a]	-0.193
Change in Hours Worked		0.854			0.138
Psychological Variables:					
Locus of Control		-1.780			-0.111
Self-Esteem	0.183	2.854[b]	0.026	8.14[b]	0.076
INTERCEPT		0.281			0.513
R Square	0.3163				
Adjusted R Square	0.2815				
F	9.085[a]				

[1] Since this part of the study incorporates changes in family size and hours worked from one year to the next as correlates, the first year of

reported results in 1980 reflects changes from 1979. [2] Beta weights are standardized multiple regression coefficients obtained when the Income-to-Poverty Ratio was regressed on all eleven predictors. [3] Uniqueness indices indicate the percentage of variance in the Income-to-Poverty Ratio accounted for by a given predictor variable beyond the variance accounted for by the other ten predictors. [4] For *t* tests that test the significance of the beta weights df = 227. [5] For F tests that tested the significance of the uniqueness indices df = 1, 227. [6] *b* is the regression coefficient, signifying by how much the IPR will change for every 1-unit change in the correlate-variable. Beta Weights and Uniqueness Indices appear only for those variables that met statistical significance.

[a] $p < .001$; [b] $p < .01$; [c] $p < .05$.

Table A.10 *Correlates of Economic Well-Being (Income-to-Poverty Ratio), 1987, Black Males (N=326)*

	Beta Weights[1]		Uniqueness Indices[2]		
CORRELATES:			Uniqueness		
Background Variables:	Beta	t[3]	Index	F[4]	*b*[5]
Age of Respondent		0.194			0.011
Highest Grade Completed, R	0.177	3.167[b]	0.024	10.03[b]	0.163
Highest Grade Completed, RM	0.106	2.051[c]	0.009	4.21[c]	0.072
Hours Worked/Year (10^{-2})	0.327	5.863[a]	0.081	34.37[a]	0.686
Marital Status (1=married)		0.012			0.002
Residence (1=within SMSA)		1.281			0.312
Unemployment Rate		-1.614			-0.196
Change Variables:					
Change in Family Size	-0.118	-2.372[b]	0.013	5.63[b]	-0.135
Change in Hours Worked		-1.098			-0.169
Psychological Variables:					
Locus of Control		-0.368			-0.023
Self-Esteem		1.929			0.045
INTERCEPT		-1.314			-2.647
R Square	0.2570				
Adjusted R Square	0.2310				
F	9.874[a]				

[1] Beta weights are standardized multiple regression coefficients obtained when the Income-to-Poverty Ratio was regressed on all

eleven predictors. [2] Uniqueness indices indicate the percentage of variance in the Income-to-Poverty Ratio accounted for by a given predictor variable beyond the variance accounted for by the other ten predictors. [3] For *t* tests that test the significance of the beta weights df = 325. [4] For F tests that tested the significance of the uniqueness indices df = 1, 325. [5] *b* is the regression coefficient, signifying by how much the IPR will change for every 1-unit change in the correlate-variable. Beta Weights and Uniqueness Indices appear only for those variables that met statistical significance.

[a] $p < .001$; [b] $p < .01$; [c] $p < .05$.

Table A.11 *Correlates of Economic Well-Being (Income-to-Poverty Ratio), 1987, White Males (N=663)*

	Beta Weights[1]	Uniqueness Indices[2]			
CORRELATES:			Uniqueness		
Background Variables:	Beta	t[3]	Index	F[4]	*b*[5]
Age of Respondent	1.730				0.105
Highest Grade Completed, R	0.211	5.370[a]	0.034	28.84[a]	0.246
Highest Grade Completed, RM		1.492			0.066
Hours Worked/Year (10^{-2})	0.229	6.033[a]	0.044	36.40[a]	0.865
Marital Status (1=married)		-0.668			-0.132
Residence (1=within SMSA)	0.115	2.896[b]	0.010	8.38[b]	0.704
Unemployment Rate	-1.103				-0.119
Change Variables:					
Change in Family Size	-0.193	-5.262[a]	0.033	27.69[a]	-0.518
Change in Hours Worked		-2.858[b]	0.010	8.17[b]	-0.515
Psychological Variables:					
Locus of Control		-1.176			-0.70
Self-Esteem		2.265[c]	0.006	5.13[c]	0.055
INTERCEPT	-2.757[b]				-5.819
R Square	0.2158				
Adjusted R Square	0.2025				
F	16.283[a]				

[1] Beta weights are standardized multiple regression coefficients obtained when the Income-to-Poverty Ratio was regressed on all

eleven predictors. [2] Uniqueness indices indicate the percentage of variance in the Income-to-Poverty Ratio accounted for by a given predictor variable beyond the variance accounted for by the other ten predictors. [3] For *t* tests that test the significance of the beta weights df = 662. [4] For F tests that tested the significance of the uniqueness indices df = 1, 662. [5] *b* is the regression coefficient, signifying by how much the IPR will change for every 1-unit change in the correlate-variable. Beta Weights and Uniqueness Indices appear only for those variables that met statistical significance.

[a] $p < .001$; [b] $p < .01$; [c] $p < .05$.

Table A.12 *Correlates of Economic Well-Being (Income-to-Poverty Ratio), 1987, Hispanic Males (N=178)*

	Beta Weights[1]		Uniqueness Indices[2]		
CORRELATES:			Uniqueness		
Background Variables:	Beta	t[3]	Index	F[4]	*b*[5]
Age of Respondent		-0.636			-0.063
Highest Grade Completed, R	0.204	2.878[b]	0.034	8.28[b]	0.204
Highest Grade Completed, RM		1.641			0.062
Hours Worked/Year (10^{-2})	0.205	2.907[b]	0.035	8.45[b]	0.600
Marital Status (1=married)		0.679			0.207
Residence (1=within SMSA)		0.007			0.003
Unemployment Rate	-0.251	-3.508[a]	0.051	12.31[a]	-0.581
Change Variables:					
Change in Family Size	-0.088	-1.342			-0.129
Change in Hours Worked		-1.231			-0.309
Psychological Variables:					
Locus of Control		-1.273			-0.120
Self-Esteem		1.759			0.074
INTERCEPT		0.473			1.566
R Square	0.3126				
Adjusted R Square	0.2671				
F	6.864[a]				

[1] Beta weights are standardized multiple regression coefficients obtained when the Income-to-Poverty Ratio was regressed on all

eleven predictors. [2] Uniqueness indices indicate the percentage of variance in the Income-to-Poverty Ratio accounted for by a given predictor variable beyond the variance accounted for by the other ten predictors. [3] For *t* tests that test the significance of the beta weights df = 177. [4] For F tests that tested the significance of the uniqueness indices df = 1, 177. [5] *b* is the regression coefficient, signifying by how much the IPR will change for every 1-unit change in the correlate-variable. Beta Weights and Uniqueness Indices appear only for those variables that met statistical significance.

[a] $p < .001$; [b] $p < .01$; [c] $p < .05$.

Table A.13 *Correlates of Economic Well-Being (Income-to-Poverty Ratio), 1987, Black Females (N=525)*

	Beta Weights[1]		Uniqueness Indices[2]		
CORRELATES:			Uniqueness		
Background Variables:	Beta	t[3]	Index	F[4]	*b*[5]
Age of Respondent		-0.321			-0.011
Highest Grade Completed, R	0.184	4.305 [a]	0.023	18.53 [a]	0.155
Highest Grade Completed, RM		0.925			0.022
Hours Worked/Year (10^{-2})	0.351	8.306 [a]	0.086	68.99 [a]	0.613
Marital Status (1=married)	0.179	4.963 [a]	0.031	24.63 [a]	0.647
Residence (1=within SMSA)		0.905			0.146
Unemployment Rate		-2.444 [b]	0.007	5.98 [b]	-0.190
Change Variables:					
Change in Family Size	-0.088	-2.476 [b]	0.008	6.03 [b]	-0.106
Change in Hours Worked	-0.085	-2.255 [c]	0.006	5.08 [c]	-0.222
Psychological Variables:					
Locus of Control	-0.095	-2.642 [b]	0.009	6.98 [b]	-0.101
Self-Esteem		1.489			0.022
INTERCEPT		0.010			0.013
R Square	0.3442				
Adjusted R Square	0.3579				
F	25.999 [a]				

[1] Beta weights are standardized multiple regression coefficients obtained when the Income-to-Poverty Ratio was regressed on all

eleven predictors. [2] Uniqueness indices indicate the percentage of variance in the Income-to-Poverty Ratio accounted for by a given predictor variable beyond the variance accounted for by the other ten predictors. [3] For *t* tests that test the significance of the beta weights df = 524. [4] For F tests that tested the significance of the uniqueness indices df = 1, 524. [5] *b* is the regression coefficient, signifying by how much the IPR will change for every 1-unit change in the correlate-variable. Beta Weights and Uniqueness Indices appear only for those variables that met statistical significance.

[a] $p < .001$; [b] $p < .01$; [c] $p < .05$.

Table A.14 *Correlates of Economic Well-Being (Income-to-Poverty Ratio), 1987, White Females (N=825)*

	Beta Weights[1]		Uniqueness Indices[2]		
CORRELATES:			Uniqueness		
Background Variables:	Beta	t[3]	Index	F[4]	*b*[5]
Age of Respondent		-0.254			-0.013
Highest Grade Completed, R	0.245	7.000[a]	0.043	49.00[a]	0.313
Highest Grade Completed, RM	0.088	2.651[b]	0.006	7.02[b]	0.100
Hours Worked/Year (10^{-2})	0.281	8.401[a]	0.063	70.58[a]	0.859
Marital Status (1=married)	0.129	4.165[a]	0.015	17.35[a]	0.762
Residence (1=within SMSA)	0.137	4.129[a]	0.015	17.04[a]	0.896
Unemployment Rate		-1.177			-0.117
Change Variables:					
Change in Family Size	-0.065	-2.117[c]	0.004	4.48[c]	-0.212
Change in Hours Worked	-0.090	-2.842[b]	0.007	8.07[b]	-0.439
Psychological Variables:					
Locus of Control		0.283			0.015
Self-Esteem	0.111	3.560[a]	0.011	12.68[a]	0.076
INTERCEPT		-3.136[b]			-5.834
R Square	0.2791				
Adjusted R Square	0.2693				
F	28.93[a]				

[1] Beta weights are standardized multiple regression coefficients obtained when the Income-to-Poverty Ratio was regressed on all

eleven predictors. [2] Uniqueness indices indicate the percentage of variance in the Income-to-Poverty Ratio accounted for by a given predictor variable beyond the variance accounted for by the other ten predictors. [3] For *t* tests that test the significance of the beta weights df = 824. [4] For F tests that tested the significance of the uniqueness indices df = 1, 824. [5] *b* is the regression coefficient, signifying by how much the IPR will change for every 1-unit change in the correlate-variable. Beta Weights and Uniqueness Indices appear only for those variables that met statistical significance.

[a] $p < .001$; [b] $p < .01$; [c] $p < .05$.

Table A.15 *Correlates of Economic Well-Being (Income-to-Poverty Ratio), 1987, Hispanic Females (N=228)*

	Beta Weights [1]		Uniqueness Indices [2]		
CORRELATES:			Uniqueness		
Background Variables:	Beta	t [3]	Index	F [4]	*b* [5]
Age of Respondent		-0.451			-0.031
Highest Grade Completed, R	0.236	3.843 [a]	0.038	9.14 [a]	0.169
Highest Grade Completed, RM		0.480			0.014
Hours Worked/Year (10^{-2})	0.374	6.064 [a]	0.095	22.76 [a]	0.835
Marital Status (1=married)	0.181	3.454 [a]	0.031	7.38 [a]	0.780
Residence (1=within SMSA)		-0.344			-0.122
Unemployment Rate	-0.160	-2.899 [b]	0.022	5.20 [b]	-0.338
Change Variables:					
Change in Family Size		-0.996			-0.076
Change in Hours Worked		-1.330			-0.278
Psychological Variables:					
Locus of Control		-1.584			-0.114
Self-Esteem	0.151	2.515 [c]	0.016	3.91 [c]	0.074
INTERCEPT		0.011			0.027
R Square	0.4402				
Adjusted R Square	0.4117				
F	15.441 [a]				

[1] Beta weights are standardized multiple regression coefficients obtained when the Income-to-Poverty Ratio was regressed on all

eleven predictors. [2] Uniqueness indices indicate the percentage of variance in the Income-to-Poverty Ratio accounted for by a given predictor variable beyond the variance accounted for by the other ten predictors. [3] For *t* tests that test the significance of the beta weights df = 227. [4] For F tests that tested the significance of the uniqueness indices df = 1, 227. [5] *b* is the regression coefficient, signifying by how much the IPR will change for every 1-unit change in the correlate-variable. Beta Weights and Uniqueness Indices appear only for those variables that met statistical significance.

[a] $p < .001$; [b] $p < .01$; [c] $p < .05$.

Table A.16 *Correlates of Economic Well-Being (Income-to-Poverty Ratio), 1993, Black Males (N=326)*

	Beta Weights[1]		Uniqueness Indices[2]		
CORRELATES:			Uniqueness		
Background Variables:	Beta	t[3]	Index	F[4]	*b*[5]
Age of Respondent		0.354			0.022
Highest Grade Completed, R	0.292	5.241[a]	0.062	27.47[a]	0.291
Highest Grade Completed, RM		1.017			0.039
Hours Worked/Year (10^{-2})	0.279	5.026[a]	0.057	25.27[a]	0.569
Marital Status (1=married)		-0.896			-0.189
Residence (1=within SMSA)		0.605			0.184
Unemployment Rate		-0.415			-0.062
Change Variables:					
Change in Family Size		-0.948			-0.086
Change in Hours Worked		-0.774			-0.128
Psychological Variables:					
Locus of Control		-0.696			-0.479
Self-Esteem		2.634[b]	0.016	6.94[b]	0.068
INTERCEPT		-1.736			-4.385
R Square	0.2966				
Adjusted R Square	0.2719				
F	12.036[a]				

[1] Beta weights are standardized multiple regression coefficients obtained when the Income-to-Poverty Ratio was regressed on all

eleven predictors. [2] Uniqueness indices indicate the percentage of variance in the Income-to-Poverty Ratio accounted for by a given predictor variable beyond the variance accounted for by the other ten predictors. [3] For *t* tests that test the significance of the beta weights df = 325. [4] For F tests that tested the significance of the uniqueness indices df = 1, 325. [5] *b* is the regression coefficient, signifying by how much the IPR will change for every 1-unit change in the correlate-variable. Beta Weights and Uniqueness Indices appear only for those variables that met statistical significance.

[a] $p < .001$; [b] $p < .01$; [c] $p < .05$.

Table A.17 *Correlates of Economic Well-Being (Income-to-Poverty Ratio), 1993, White Males (N=663)*

	Beta Weights[1]		Uniqueness Indices[2]		
CORRELATES:			Uniqueness		
Background Variables:	Beta	t[3]	Index	F[4]	*b*[5]
Age of Respondent		1.268			0.066
Highest Grade Completed, R	0.260	6.577[a]	0.053	43.26[a]	0.247
Highest Grade Completed, RM		1.175			0.045
Hours Worked/Year (10^{-2})	0.187	4.671[a]	0.027	21.82[a]	0.580
Marital Status (1=married)	-0.106	-2.816[b]	0.010	7.93[b]	-0.517
Residence (1=within SMSA)	0.202	5.435[a]	0.036	29.54[a]	1.081
Unemployment Rate		0.630			0.066
Change Variables:					
Change in Family Size		-1.238			-0.135
Change in Hours Worked		-0.266			-0.046
Psychological Variables:					
Locus of Control		-0.867			-0.044
Self-Esteem		1.825			0.039
INTERCEPT		-2.275[c]			-4.668
R Square	0.2045				
Adjusted R Square	0.1911				
F	15.218[a]				

[1] Beta weights are standardized multiple regression coefficients obtained when the Income-to-Poverty Ratio was regressed on all

eleven predictors. [2] Uniqueness indices indicate the percentage of variance in the Income-to-Poverty Ratio accounted for by a given predictor variable beyond the variance accounted for by the other ten predictors. [3] For *t* tests that test the significance of the beta weights df = 622. [4] For F tests that tested the significance of the uniqueness indices df = 1, 622. [5] *b* is the regression coefficient, signifying by how much the IPR will change for every 1-unit change in the correlate-variable. Beta Weights and Uniqueness Indices appear only for those variables that met statistical significance.

[a] $p < .001$; [b] $p < .01$; [c] $p < .05$.

Table A.18 *Correlates of Economic Well-Being (Income-to-Poverty Ratio), 1993, Hispanic Males (N=178)*

	Beta Weights [1]		Uniqueness Indices [2]		
CORRELATES:			Uniqueness		
Background Variables:	Beta	t [3]	Index	F [4]	*b* [5]
Age of Respondent		-0.628			-0.063
Highest Grade Completed, R	0.265	3.202 [b]	0.051	10.25 [b]	0.219
Highest Grade Completed, RM		0.413			0.016
Hours Worked/Year (10^{-2})		1.667			0.381
Marital Status (1=married)		0.561			0.185
Residence (1=within SMSA)		1.738			1.008
Unemployment Rate		-1.111			-0.171
Change Variables:					
Change in Family Size		-0.223			-0.037
Change in Hours Worked		1.047			0.324
Psychological Variables:					
Locus of Control		-0.417			-0.041
Self-Esteem		0.683			0.028
INTERCEPT		0.298			1.116
R Square	0.1731				
Adjusted R Square	0.1183				
F	3.159 [a]				

[1] Beta weights are standardized multiple regression coefficients obtained when the Income-to-Poverty Ratio was regressed on all

eleven predictors. [2] Uniqueness indices indicate the percentage of variance in the Income-to-Poverty Ratio accounted for by a given predictor variable beyond the variance accounted for by the other ten predictors. [3] For *t* tests that test the significance of the beta weights df = 177. 4 For F tests that tested the significance of the uniqueness indices df = 1, 177. [5] *b* is the regression coefficient, signifying by how much the IPR will change for every 1-unit change in the correlate-variable. Beta Weights and Uniqueness Indices appear only for those variables that met statistical significance.

[a] $p < .001$; [b] $p < .01$; [c] $p < .05$.

Table A.19 *Correlates of Economic Well-Being (Income-to-Poverty Ratio), 1993, Black Females (N=525)*

	Beta Weights[1]	Uniqueness Indices[2]			
CORRELATES:			Uniqueness		
Background Variables:	Beta	t[3]	Index	F[4]	b[5]
Age of Respondent		1.284			0.048
Highest Grade Completed, R	0.285	6.716[a]	0.057	45.11[a]	0.225
Highest Grade Completed, RM		0.930			0.022
Hours Worked/Year (10^{-2})	0.339	8.111[a]	0.082	65.79[a]	0.549
Marital Status (1=married)	0.128	3.542[a]	0.016	12.55[a]	0.467
Residence (1=within SMSA)		-0.021			-0.003
Unemployment Rate		-0.225			-0.019
Change Variables:					
Change in Family Size	-0.079	-2.219[c]	0.006	4.92[c]	-0.146
Change in Hours Worked		-1.613			-0.169
Psychological Variables:					
Locus of Control	-0.770	-2.130[c]	0.006	4.53[c]	-0.083
Self-Esteem		1.392			0.216
INTERCEPT		-2.117[c]			-3.089
R Square	0.3568				
Adjusted R Square	0.3430				
F	25.867[a]				

[1] Beta weights are standardized multiple regression coefficients obtained when the Income-to-Poverty Ratio was regressed on all

eleven predictors. [2] Uniqueness indices indicate the percentage of variance in the Income-to-Poverty Ratio accounted for by a given predictor variable beyond the variance accounted for by the other ten predictors. [3] For *t* tests that test the significance of the beta weights df = 524. [4] For F tests that tested the significance of the uniqueness indices df = 1, 524. [5] *b* is the regression coefficient, signifying by how much the IPR will change for every 1-unit change in the correlate-variable. Beta Weights and Uniqueness Indices appear only for those variables that met statistical significance.

[a] $p < .001$; [b] $p < .01$; [c] $p < .05$.

Table A.20 *Correlates of Economic Well-Being (Income-to-Poverty Ratio), 1993, White Females (N=825)*

	Beta Weights[1]	Uniqueness Indices[2]			
CORRELATES:			Uniqueness		
Background Variables:	Beta	t[3]	Index	F[4]	*b*[5]
Age of Respondent		-0.459			-0.018
Highest Grade Completed, R	0.337	10.004[a]	0.086	100.09[a]	0.317
Highest Grade Completed, RM		1.921			0.055
Hours Worked/Year (10^{-2})	0.293	9.151[a]	0.072	83.75[a]	0.669
Marital Status (1=married)		1.961			0.290
Residence (1=within SMSA)	0.152	4.801[a]	0.020	23.06[a]	0.783
Unemployment Rate		0.028			0.002
Change Variables:					
Change in Family Size		-0.326			-0.032
Change in Hours Worked		-2.512[c]	0.005	6.31[c]	-0.304
Psychological Variables:					
Locus of Control		-0.792			-0.033
Self-Esteem		1.503			0.024
INTERCEPT		-1.674			-2.703
R Square	0.3037				
Adjusted R Square	0.2943				
F	32.236[a]				

[1] Beta weights are standardized multiple regression coefficients obtained when the Income-to-Poverty Ratio was regressed on all eleven predictors. [2] Uniqueness indices indicate the percentage of

variance in the Income-to-Poverty Ratio accounted for by a given predictor variable beyond the variance accounted for by the other ten predictors. [3] For *t* tests that test the significance of the beta weights df = 824. [4] For F tests that tested the significance of the uniqueness indices df = 1, 824. [5] *b* is the regression coefficient, signifying by how much the IPR will change for every 1-unit change in the correlate-variable. Beta Weights and Uniqueness Indices appear only for those variables that met statistical significance.

[a] $p < .001$; [b] $p < .01$; [c] $p < .05$.

Table A.21 *Correlates of Economic Well-Being (Income-to-Poverty Ratio), 1993, Hispanic Females (N=228)*

	Beta Weights[1]		Uniqueness Indices[2]		
CORRELATES:			Uniqueness		
Background Variables:	Beta	t[3]	Index	F[4]	*b*[5]
Age of Respondent		-0.646			-0.042
Highest Grade Completed, R	0.273	4.294[a]	0.054	18.44[a]	0.168
Highest Grade Completed, RM		1.636			0.044
Hours Worked/Year (10^{-2})	0.317	5.180[a]	0.078	26.84[a]	0.612
Marital Status (1=married)	0.125	2.254[c]	0.015	5.08[c]	0.481
Residence (1=within SMSA)		0.946			0.351
Unemployment Rate		-0.278			-0.028
Change Variables:					
Change in Family Size		-0.448			-0.061
Change in Hours Worked		-1.746			-0.339
Psychological Variables:					
Locus of Control		-1.218			-0.080
Self-Esteem		1.959			0.053
INTERCEPT		-0.069			-0.175
R Square	0.3714				
Adjusted R Square	0.3394				
F	11.603[a]				

[1] Beta weights are standardized multiple regression coefficients obtained when the Income-to-Poverty Ratio was regressed on all eleven predictors. [2] Uniqueness indices indicate the percentage of

variance in the Income-to-Poverty Ratio accounted for by a given predictor variable beyond the variance accounted for by the other ten predictors. [3] For *t* tests that test the significance of the beta weights df = 227. [4] For F tests that tested the significance of the uniqueness indices df = 1, 227. [5] *b* is the regression coefficient, signifying by how much the IPR will change for every 1-unit change in the correlate-variable. Beta Weights and Uniqueness Indices appear only for those variables that met statistical significance.

[a] $p < .001$; [b] $p < .01$; [c] $p < .05$.

REFERENCES

Anderson, M. (1988). *Revolution.* San Diego, CA: Harcourt Brace Jovanovich, Publishers.

Armey, D. (1995). *The freedom revolution.* Washington, DC: Regnery Publishing, Inc.

Baily, M.N., Burtless, G., and Litan, R.E. (1993). *Growth with equity: Economic policymaking for the next century.* Washington, DC: Brookings Institution.

Barbour, H. (1996). *Agenda for America: A republican direction for the future.* Washington, DC: Regnery Publishing, Inc.

Bartlett, D.L. and Steele, J.B. (1992). *America: What went wrong,* Kansas City, MO: Andrews and McMeel.

Bassi, L.J. (1995). Stimulating employment and increasing opportunity for the current work force. In D.S. Nightingale and R.H. Haveman (Eds.), *The work alternative,* pp. 137-156. Washington, DC: The Urban Institute Press.

Berry, M.F. (1996). Affirmative action: Why we need it, why it is under attack. In G.E.Curry (Ed.), *The affirmative action debate,* pp. 299-313. Reading, MA: Addison-Wesley Publishing Company.

Berryman, S. (1988). *Literacy and the marketplace: Improving the literacy of low income single mothers.* New York: The Rockefeller Foundation.

Blank, R.M. (1997). *It takes a nation: A new agenda for fighting poverty.* New York: Russell Sage Foundation / Princeton, NJ: Princeton University Press.

Blank, R.M. (1995). Outlook for the US labor market and prospects for low-wage entry jobs. In D.S. Nightingale and R.H. Haveman (Eds.), *The work alternative*, pp. 33-69. Washington, DC: The Urban Institute Press.

Blank, R.M. (1994). The employment strategy: Public policies to increase work and earnings. In S.H. Danziger, G.D. Sandefur, and D.H. Weinberg (Eds.), *Confronting poverty: Prescriptions for change.* New York: Russell Sage Foundation / Cambridge, MA: Harvard University Press.

Block, F.L. (1996). *The vampire state and other myths and fallacies about the US economy*. New York: The New Press.

Bok, D. (1994). *The cost of talent: How executives and professionals are paid and how it affects America*. New York: The Free Press.

Boor, M. (1974). Dimensions of internal-external control and marital status, sex, age, and college class. *Journal of Social Psychology*, 94, 145-146.

Burggraf, S.P. (1997). *The feminine economy and economic man: Reviving the role of family in the postindustrial age*. Reading, MA: Addison-Wesley Publishing Company, Inc.

Burghardt, J. and Gordon, A. (1990). *More jobs and higher pay: How an integrated program compares with traditional programs*. New York: The Rockefeller Foundation.

Burtless, G. (1995). Employment prospects of welfare recipients. In D.S. Nightingale and R.H. Haveman (Eds.), *The work alternative*, pp. 71-106. Washington, DC: The Urban Institute Press.

Burtless, G. (1985). Are targeted wage subsidies harmful? Evidence from a wage voucher experiment. *Industrial and Labor Relations Review*, 39(1), 105-114.

Burton, C.E. (1992). *The poverty debate: Politics and the poor in America*. Westport, CT: Praeger.

Caputo, R.K. (1999). Becoming poor and using public assistance programs. *Journal of Poverty*, 3, 1-23.

Caputo, R.K. (1998). Economic well-being in a youth cohort. *Families in Society*, 79, 83-92.

Caputo, R.K. (1997a). Escaping poverty and becoming self-sufficient. *Journal of Sociology and Social Welfare*, 24(3), 5-23.

Caputo, R.K. (1997b). Family poverty and public dependency. *Families in Society*, 78, 13-25.

Caputo, R.K. (1997c). Psychological, attitudinal, and socio-demographic correlates of economic well-being of mature women. *Journal of Women and Aging*, 9(4), 37-53.

Caputo, R.K. (1995a). Gender and race: Employment opportunity and the American economy. *Families in Society*, 76, 239-247.

Caputo, R.K. (1995b). Income inequality and family poverty. *Families in Society*, 76, 604-615.

Caputo, R.K. (1994). *Welfare and freedom American style II: The role of the federal government*, 1941-1980. Lanham, MD: University Press of America.

Caputo, R.K. and Cianni, M.A. (1997). Job training experiences of black and white women, 1970-1991. *Human Resource Development Quarterly*, 8, 197-217.

Card, D. and Krueger, A.B. (1995). *Myth and measurement: The new economics of the minimum wage*. Princeton, NJ: Princeton University Press.

Carnoy, M. (1994). *Faded dreams: The politics and economics of race in America*. Cambridge, Eng.: Cambridge University Press.

Center for Human Resource Research. (1995). *NLS Handbook* 1995. Columbus: Ohio State University.

Chase, E.T. (1997, October 13). Market value-free. Book review of E.S. Phelps, *Rewarding work: How to restore participation and self-support to free enterprise*. Cambridge, MA: Harvard University Press, 1997. *The Nation*, 30-31.

Clinton, W.J. (1997a, June 13). Executive order 13050-President's advisory board on race. *Weekly compilation of presidential documents*, 33, 873-874.

Clinton, W.J. (1997b, June 14). Remarks at the University of California San Diego commencement ceremony in LaJolla, California. *Weekly compilation of presidential documents*, 33, 876-882.

Clinton, W.J. (1995a, July 19). Memorandum on affirmative action. *Weekly compilation of presidential documents*, 31, 1264-1265.

Clinton, W.J. (1995b, July 19). Remarks at the national archives and records administration. *Weekly compilation of presidential documents*, 31, 1255-1264.

Cody, R.P. and Smith, J.K. (1997). *Applied statistics and the SAS programming language*. Fourth edition; Upper Saddle River, NJ: Prentice Hall.

Coe, R.D. (1981). A preliminary empirical examination of the dynamics of welfare use. In M.S. Hill and J.N. Morgan (Eds.), *Five thousand American families - patterns of economic progress*, Vol. 9; Ann Arbor: Institute for Social Research, The University of Michigan.

Committee on Ways and Means. U.S. House of Representatives (1996). *1996 Green Book*: Background material and data on programs within the jurisdiction of the committee on ways and means. Washington, DC: Government Printing Office.

Coontz, S. (1997). *The way we really are: Coming to terms with America's changing families*. New York: Basic Books.

CQ 1997 Almanac (1998). No agreement on training bills. *Congressional Quarterly Almanac*, 53, 7-18 - 7-21. Washington, DC:

Congressional Quarterly Inc.

CQ 1996 Almanac (1997a). Welfare overhaul after 60 years, most control sent to states. *Congressional Quarterly Almanac*, 52, 6-3 - 6-24. Washington, DC: Congressional Quarterly Inc.

CQ 1996 Almanac (1997b). Tax breaks sweeten wage increase. *Congressional Quarterly Almanac*, 52, 2-34 - 2-39. Washington, DC: Congressional Quarterly Inc.

CQ 1994 Almanac (1995). Clinton signs school-to-work bill. *Congressional Quarterly Almanac*, 50, 400-401. Washington, DC: Congressional Quarterly Inc.

CQ 1993 Almanac (1994). 1993 budget reconciliation act. *Congressional Quarterly Almanac*, 49, 124-139. Washington, DC: Congressional Quarterly Inc.

Danziger, S. and Gottschalk, P. (1995) *America unequal*. New York: Russell Sage Foundation / Cambridge, MA: Harvard University Press.

Danziger, S. and Gottschalk, P., (Eds.). (1993). *Uneven tides: Rising inequality in America*. New York: Russell Sage Foundation.

Danziger, S., Sandefur, G.D., and Weinberg, D.H. (Eds.). (1994). *Confronting poverty: Prescriptions for change*. New York: Russell Sage Foundation / Cambridge, MA: Harvard University Press.

Darby, M.R. (Ed.). (1996). *Reducing poverty in America: Views and approaches*. Thousand Oaks, CA: Sage Publications.

Davidson, C. and Woodbury, S.A. (1993). The displacement effects of reemployment bonus programs. *Journal of Labor Economics*, 11(4), 575-605.

Disney, R. (1996). *Can we afford to grow older: A perspective on the economics of aging*. Cambridge, MA: The MIT Press.

Dolinsky, A.L., Caputo, R.K, and O'Kane, P. (1989). Competing effects of culture and situation on welfare receipt. *Social Service Review*, 63, 359-371.

Dolinsky, A.L., Caputo, R.K., and Pasumarty, K. (1994). Long-term entrepreneurship patterns: A national study of black and white female entry and stayer status differences. *Journal of Small Business Management*, 32(1), 18-26.

Duncan, G.J. (1984). *Years of poverty years of plenty: The changing economic fortunes of American workers and families*. Ann Arbor, MI: Institute for Social Research, University of Michigan.

Duncan, G.J., Boisjoly, J., and Smeeding, T. (1997, April 14). How long does it take a young worker to support a family? Evanston, IL: Northwestern University Policy Research, Department of Political Science
(http://www.library.nwu.edu/publications/nupr/duncan.html).

Duncan, G.J., Gustafsson, B., Hauser, R., Schmaus, G., Jenkins, S., Messinger, H., Muffels, R., Nolan, B., Ray, J-C., and Voges, W. (1995). Poverty and social assistance dynamics in the United States, Canada, and Europe. In K. McFate, R. Lawson, and W.J. Wilson (Eds.), *Poverty, inequality, and the future of social policy*, pp. 67-108. New York: Russell Sage Foundation.

Duncan, G.J. and Brooks-Gunn, J., Eds. (1997). *Consequences of growing up poor*. New York: Russell Sage Foundation.

D'Souza, D. (1995). *The end of racism*. New York: The Free Press.

Economic Conference. (1992). *President Clinton's new beginning*. New York: Donald I. Fine.

Economic report of the president (1997). Washington, DC: Government Printing Office.

Edin, K. and Lein, L. (1997). *Making ends meet: How single mothers survive welfare and low-wage work*. New York: Russell Sage Foundation.

Franklin, D.L. (1997). *Ensuring inequality: The structural transformation of the African-American family*. New York: Oxford University Press.

Galbraith, J.K. (1998). *Created unequal: The crisis in American pay*. New York: The Free Press.

Gingrich, N. (1995) *To renew America*. New York: HarperCollins Publishers.

Goodwin, L. (1983). *Causes and cures of welfare: New evidence on the social psychology of the poor*. Lexington, MA.: Lexington Books/D.C. Heath and Company.

Gordon, S. (1980). *Welfare, justice, and freedom*. New York: Columbia University Press.

Gottschalk, P., Mchanahan, S., and Sandefur, G.D. (1994). The dynamics and intergenerational transmission of poverty and welfare particiation. In S. H. Danziger, G. D. Sandefur, and D. H. Weinberg (Eds.), Confronting poverty: Prescriptions for change, pp. 85-108. Cambridge, MA: Harvard University Press.

Greenberg, S.B. (1995). *Middle class dreams: The politics and power of the new American majority*. New York: Times Books/Random House.

Greenberg, S.B. and Skocpol, T. (1997a). Democratic possibilities. *The American Prospect*, 35 (November-December), 34-38.

Greenberg, S.B. and Skocpol, T. (1997b). *The new majority: Toward a popular progressive politics*. New Haven, CT: Yale University Press.

Grubb, W.N. (1996). *Learning to work: The case for reintegrating job training and education*. New York: Russell Sage Foundation.

Gueron, J.M. (1996). Welfare and poverty: Strategies to increase work. In M.R. Darby (Ed.), *Reducing poverty in America: Views and approaches*, pp. 235-250. Thousand Oaks, CA: Sage Publications.

Hacker, A. (1992). *Two nations: Black and white, separate, hostile, unequal*. New York: Charles Scribner's Sons.

Hartmann, H. (1996). Who has benefited from affirmative action in employment? In G.E. Curry (Ed.), *The affirmative action debate*, pp. 77-

96. Reading, MA: Addison-Wesley Publishing Company.

Hatcher, L. and Stepanski, E.J. (1994). *A step-by-step approach to using the SAS system for univariate and multivariate statistics.* Cary, NC: SAS Institute, Inc.

Haveman, R.H. (1995). The Clinton alternative to "welfare as we know it": Is it feasible? In D.S. Nightingale and R.H. Haveman (Eds.), *The work alternative*, pp. 185-202. Washington, DC: The Urban Institute Press.

Haveman, R.H. and Buron, L. (1993). Escaping poverty through work: The problem of low earnings capacity in the United States, 1973-1988. *Review of Income and Wealth*, 39, 141-157.

Hernandez, D.J. (1997). Poverty trends. In G.J. Duncan and J. Brooks-Gunn (Eds.), *Consequences of growing up poor*, pp. 18-34. New York: Russell Sage Foundation.

Hollister, R., Kemper, P., and Maynard, R.A. (1984). *The national supported work demonstration*. Madison: University of Wisconsin Press.

Houseman, S.N. (1998). The effects of employer mandates. In R.B. Freeman and P. Gottschalk (Eds.), *Generating jobs: How to increase demand for less-skilled workers*, pp. 154-191. New York: Russell Sage Foundation.

Howard, C. (1997). T*he hidden welfare state: Tax expenditures and social policy in the United States*. Princeton, NJ: Princeton University Press.

H.R. 1385 (1998). Bill summary and status for the 105th Congress. (http://thomas.loc.gov/cgi-bin/bdquery/z?d105:HRO1385:@@@L)

Jencks, C. (1996). Can we replace welfare with work? In M.R. Darby (Ed.), *Reducing poverty in America: Views and approaches,* pp. 69-81. Thousand Oaks, CA: Sage Publications.

Joe, V.C. (1971). Review of the internal-external construct as a personality variable. *Psychological Reports*, 28, 619-640.

Johnson, J.H. (1996). The real issues for reducing poverty. In M.R. Darby (Ed.), *Reducing poverty in America: Views and approaches*, pp. 337-363. Thousand Oaks, CA: Sage Publications.

Jones, J. (1998). American work: Four centuries of black and white labor. New York: W.W. Norton and Company.

Jones, J. (1985). *Labor of love, labor of sorrow: Black women, work, and the family from slavery to the present*. New York: Basic Books, Inc.

Karoly, L.A. (1993). The trend in inequality among families, individuals, and workers in the United States: A twenty-five year perspective. In S. Danziger and P. Gottschalk (Eds.), *Uneven tides: Rising inequality in America*, pp. 19-97. New York: Russell Sage Foundation.

Katz, J.L. (1997, October 25). Long-term challenges temper cheers for welfare successes. *Congressional Quarterly Weekly Report*, 55, 2603-2610.

Katz, J.L. (1996, September 21). Provisions welfare overhaul law. *Congressional Quarterly Weekly Report*, 54, 2696-2705.

Katz, M.B. (1989). T*he undeserving poor: From the war on poverty to the war on welfare*. Cambridge, MA: The MIT Press.

Kelso, W.A. (1994). *Poverty and the underclass: Changing perceptions of the poor in America*. NY: New York University Press.

Kozol, J. (1991). *Savage inequalities: Children in America's schools*. New York: HarperCollins Publishers.

Krugman, P. (1997, November 3). Superiority complex. *The New Republic*, 20-21.

Krugman, P. (1992). *The age of diminished expectations: US economic policy in the 1990s*. Cambridge, MA: The MIT Press.

Lerman, R.L. (1996). *Building hope, skills, and careers: Creating a youth apprenticeship system*. In I. Garfinkel, J.L. Hochschild, and S.S. McLanahan (Eds.), Social policies for children, pp. 136-172. Washington, DC: The Brookings Institution.

Levy, F. (1995). Incomes and income inequality. In R. Farley (Ed.), *State of the union: America in the 1990s,* Vol. I, *Economic trends,* pp. 1-57. II Vols.; New York: Russell Sage Foundation.

Levy, F. and Michel, R.C. (1991). *The economic future of American families: Income and wealth trends*. Washington, DC: The Urban Institute Press.

Lieberson, S. (1985). *Making it count: The improvement of social research and theory*. Berkeley: University of California Press.

Loury, G.C. (1996). A dissent from the incentive approaches to reducing poverty. In M.R. Darby (Ed.), *Reducing poverty in America: Views and approaches*, pp. 111-117. Thousand Oaks, CA: Sage Publications.

Lynch, L.M. (1989). Private sector training and its impact on the earnings of young workers. National Bureau of Economic Research Working Paper Series 2872. Washington, DC: National Bureau of Economic Research.

Madrick, J. (1995). *The end of affluence: The causes and consequences of America's economic dilemma*. New York: Random House.

Maxfield, M. (1988). Characteristics employers prefer in unskilled job applicants. Washington, DC: Greater Washington Research Center.

Maynard, R.A. (1995). Subsidized employment and non-labor market alternatives for welfare recipients. In D.S. Nightingale and R.H. Haveman (Eds.), *The work alternative*, pp. 109-136. Washington, DC: The Urban Institute Press.

Maynard, R.A., Nichelson, W., and Rangarajan, A. (1992). *Breaking the cycle of poverty: The effectiveness of mandatory services for welfare-dependent teenage parents*. Princeton: Mathmatica Policy Research, Inc.

McFate, K., Lawson, R., and Wilson, W.J. (Eds.). (1995). *Poverty, inequality, and the future of social policy*. New York: Russell Sage Foundation.

McLanahan, S. and Casper, L. (1995). Growing diversity and inequality in the American family. In R. Farley (Ed.), *State of the union: America in the 1990s*, Vol. II, *Social trends*, pp. 1-45. II Vols.; New York: Russell Sage Foundation.

McLanahan, S. and Garfinkel, I. (1997). *Single mother families and social policy: Lessons for the United States from Canada, France, and Sweden*. In K. McFate, R. Lawson, and W.J. Wilson (Eds.), Poverty, inequality, and the future of social policy, pp. 367-383. New York: Russell Sage Foundation.

McLanahan, S. and Sandefur, G. (1994). *Growing up with a single parent: What hurts, what helps*. Cambridge, MA: Harvard University Press.

McMurrer, D. (1993). Reemployment bonuses: Summary. Report prepared for the Advisory Council on Unemployment Compensation. U.S. Department of Labor, Washington, DC. Draft.

Mead, L.M. (1996). Raising work levels among the poor. In M.R. Darby (Ed.), *Reducing poverty in America: Views and approaches*, pp. 251-282. Thousand Oaks, CA: Sage Publications.

Menaghan, E.G. (1990). The impact of occupational and economic pressures on young mothers' self-esteem: Evidence from the NLSY. Presented: Annual Meetings of the Society for the Study of Social Problems, Washington, DC., August 9.

Moore, R.W. and Blake, D. (1992). Does ETP training work? *An analysis of the economic outcomes of California employment training panel programs*. Northridge: California State University, Northridge School of Business Administration and Economics.

Moore, R.W., Wilms, W.W., and Bolus, R.E. (1988). *Training for change: An analysis of the outcomes of California employment training panel programs*. Santa Monica: Training Research Corporation.

Mowry, G.E. and Brownell, B.A. (1981). *The urban nation 1920-1980.* Revised edition; New York: Hill and Wang.

Murnane, R.J. and Levy, F. (1996). *Teaching the new basic skills: Principles for educating children to thrive in a changing economy.* New York: Martin Kessler Books/The Free Press.

Murray, C. (1996). Reducing poverty and reducing the underclass: Different problems, different solutions. In M.R. Darby (Ed.), *Reducing poverty in America: Views and approaches*, pp. 82-110. Thousand Oaks, CA: Sage Publications.

Murray, C. (1984). *Losing ground*. New York: Basic Books.

Newman, K.S. (1993). *Declining fortunes: The withering of the American dream*. New York: Basic Books.

Newman, K.S. (1988). *Falling from grace: The experience of downward mobility in the American middle class*. New York: Vintage Books.

Nightingale, D.M. and Haveman, R.H. (1995). *The work alternative: Welfare reform and the realities of the job market*. Washington, DC: The Urban Institute Press.

Olson, L. (1997). *The work-to-school revolution*. Reading, MA: Addison-Wesley.

Ozawa, M.N. (1995). The economic status of vulnerable older women. *Social Work*, 40, 323-331.

Palmer, J.L. and Barth, M.C. (1978). *The distributional effects of inflation and higher unemployment*. Washington, DC: Brookings Institution.

Phelps, E.S. (1997). *Rewarding work: How to restore participation and self-support to free enterprise*. Cambridge, MA: Harvard University Press.

Phillips, K.P. (1993). *Boiling point: Democrats, Republicans, and the decline of middle-class prosperity*. New York: Random House.

Phillips, K.P. (1990). *The politics of rich and poor: Wealth and the American electorate in the Reagan aftermath*. New York: Random House.

Popenoe, D. (1990). Family decline in America. In D. Blankenhorn, S. Bayme, and J.B. Elshtain (Eds.), *Rebuilding the nest: A new commitment to the American family*, pp. 39-51. Milwaukee, WI: Family Service America.

Pouncy, H. and Mincy, R.B. (1995). Out-of-welfare strategies for welfare-bound youth. In D.S. Nightingale and R.H. Haveman (Eds.), *The work alternative*, pp. 157-182. Washington, DC: The Urban Institute Press.

Rangarajan, A., Kiskar, E.E., and Maynard, R.A. (1992). *Selecting basic skills tests for program and evaluation purposes*. Princeton, NJ: Mathmatica Policy Research, Inc.

Rawls, J. (1971). *A theory of justice*. Cambridge, MA: Harvard University Press.

Rawls, J. (1993). *Political liberalism*. New York: Columbia University Press.

Reed, B. (1997). In whose interests? White women and the campaign against affirmative action. *Sojourner*, 22(12), (http://208.194.155.124/cgi-bin/cwisearch.exe?id=18324andsk =ijlmhdjqlgpihkpehsgpefopjfsqojok 10/20/97), 4 pages.

Reich, R.B. (1997). *Locked in the cabinet*. New York: Alfred A. Knopf.

Rescher, N. (1966). *Distributive justice*. Indianapolis, IN: Bobbs-Merrill Co.

Rifkin, R.L. (1995). *The end of work: The decline of the global labor force and the dawn of the post-market era*. New York: G.P. Putnam's Sons, a Jeremy P. Tarcher / Putnam Book.

Rodgers, H.R. (1990). *Poor women, poor families: The economic plight of America's female-headed households*. Revised edition; Armonk, NY: M.E. Sharpe, Inc.

Rosenberg, M. (1965). *Society and the adolescent self-image*. Princeton, NJ: Princeton University Press.

Rotter, J.B. (1966) Generalized expectations for internal versus external control reinforcement. *Psychological Monographs General and Applied*, 80, 1-28.

Rotter, J.B. (1975). Some problems and misconceptions related to the construct of internal versus external control of reinforcement. *Journal of Consulting and Clinical Psychology*, 43, 56-67.

Rubin, A. and Babbie, E. (1997). *Research methods for social work*. Third edition; Pacific Grove, CA: Brooks/Cole Publishing Company.

Rubin, A.J. (1996, August 3). Congress clears wage increase with tax breaks for business. *Congressional Quarterly Weekly Report*, 54, 2175-2177.

Rubin, A.J. and Weisman, J. (1996, September 21). Tax cut, minimum wage law. *Congressional Quarterly Weekly Report*, 54, 2705-2708.

Rubin, L.B. (1994). *Families on the fault line*. New York: HarperCollins Publishers.

Ruggles, P. (1990). *Drawing the line: Alternative poverty measures and their implications for public policy*. Washington, DC: The Urban Institute Press.

Schwarz, J.E. (1997). *Illusions of opportunity: The American dream in question*. New York: W.W. Norton and Company.

Simms, M.C. (1996). Training, work, and poverty. In M.R. Darby (Ed.), *Reducing poverty in America: Views and approaches,* pp. 283-289. Thousand Oaks, CA: Sage Publications.

Social Security Administration (1995). *Annual statistical supplement, 1995*, to the *Social Security Bulletin*. Washington, DC: U.S. Government Printing Office.

Steinberg, S. (1995). *Turning back: The retreat from racial justice in American thought and policy*. Boston: Beacon Press.

Stevens, J. (1986). *Applied multivariate statistics for the social sciences.* Hillsdale, NJ: Lawrence Erlbaum Associates, Publishers.

Strain, M. and Kisler, E.E. (1989, August). *Literacy and the disadvantaged: Analysis of data from the national assessment of education progress.* Princeton, NJ: Mathmatica Policy Research, Inc.

Strocchia-Rivera, L. (1988). Self-esteem and educational aspirations as antecedents of adolescent unmarried motherhood. Ph.D. dissertation, The University of Texas at Austin.

Thernstrom, S. and Thernstrom, A. (1997). *America in black and white: One nation, indivisible.* New York: Simon and Schuster.

Tilly, C. (1996). *Half a job: Bad and good part-time jobs in a changing labor market.* Philadelphia: Temple University Press.

U.S. Bureau of the Census (1997). *Poverty in the United States: 1996.* Washington, DC: U.S. Government Printing Office.

U.S. Department of Labor (1965). *The Negro family: The case for national action.* Washington, DC: U.S. Government Printing Office.

Watson, J.M. (1981). A note on the dimensionality of the Rotter locus of control scale. *Australian Journal of Psychology*, 33, 319-330.

Webster, A. (1992). *Applied statistics for business and economics.* Instructor's edition; Homewood, IL: Irwin, Inc.

Weisberg, J. (1996). *In defense of government: The fall and rise of public trust*. New York: Scribner.

Weitzman, L.J. (1988). *Women and children last: The social and economic consequences of divorce law reform*. In S.M. Dordbusch and M.H. Strober (Eds.) Feminism, children and the new families, pp. 212 - 248. New York: The Guildford Press.

Wilson, J.B., Ellwood, D.T., and Brooks-Gunn, J. (1995). Welfare-to-work through the eyes of children. In P.L. Chase-Lansdale and J. Brooks-Gunn (Eds.), *Escape from poverty: What makes a difference for children?*, pp. 63-86. New York: Cambridge University Press.

Wilson, W.J. (1996). *When work disappears: The world of the new urban poor*. New York: Alfred A. Knopf.

Wilson, W.J. (1987). *The truly disadvantaged: The inner city, the underclass, and public policy*. Chicago: University of Chicago Press.

Wolman, W. and Colamosca, A. (1997). *The Judas economy: The triumph of capital and the betrayal of work*. Reading, MA: Addison-Wesley Publishing Company.

Woodson, R.L. (1996). Personal responsibility. In G.E. Curry (Ed.), *The affirmative action debate*, pp. 111-120. Reading, MA: Addison-Wesley Publishing Company.

Woodson, R.L. (1987). *On the road to economic freedom: An agenda for black progress*. Washington, DC: Regnery Gateway.

Zill, N., Moore, K., and Stief, T. (1991). *Welfare mothers as potential employees: A statistical profile based on national survey data.* Washington, DC: Child Trends, Inc.

Zill, N. and Nord, C.W. (1994). *Running in place: How American families are faring in a changing economy and an individualistic society.* Washington, DC: Child Trends, Inc.